Why
We
PLAY

BOOKS BY JOANNA FORTUNE

15-Minute Parenting 0–7 Years
15-Minute Parenting 8–12 Years
15-Minute Parenting the Teenage Years

Why We PLAY

How to find joy and meaning in everyday life

JOANNA FORTUNE

Thread

Published by Thread in 2022

An imprint of Storyfire Ltd.
Carmelite House
50 Victoria Embankment
London EC4Y 0DZ

www.thread-books.com

ISBN: 978-1-80314-516-7
eBook ISBN: 9-781-80314-515-0

This book is dedicated to Anne Fortune (Aunty), the best adult friend any child could have had

TABLE OF CONTENTS

INTRODUCTION

I was walking around a shop recently when I happened on a packet of water balloons. *OH MY GOD, WATER BALLOONS!* I heard myself exclaim to no one in particular. A picture vivid in detail and emotional resonance came to mind immediately. I am nine years old, drenched to my skin, howling with laughter as I race away in excited terror while my mother chases me with a water balloon, while she is also soaked to the skin. This was one of our huge family water-balloon fights, and this memory includes visiting family friends and their kids too. There must have been ten of us kids and about five adults all fully immersed in the strategies of water-balloon fights. It is a memory so alive for me that it could have happened last month, not decades ago. It was with a broad smile and a happy heart that I bought those water balloons in the shop and took them home to play with that weekend.

Think back to your own childhood and find a memory of you at your most joyful. Hold in mind what you were doing and how, in that moment, nothing else mattered and time stood still for joy. Perhaps it wasn't safe for you to play in this way and your beautiful silliness was ridiculed and short-circuited by others in your life. We all have a personal play narrative and it doesn't have to stay as history. You still have that playful self within you, and tending to and nurturing it in adulthood is one of the best personal investments you can make.

This is a book about play, specifically the role of play in our adult lives. I am going to talk about why play is integral to living a meaningful and connected life, and I am also including lots of practical invitations to play as well. In some chapters, I have included longer lists of activities so that you can read and select one that feels comfortable to start with or perhaps gradually work your way through the list. In other places, such as between sections and chapters, I have included what I call 'play breaks' that are intended to serve as mini-pauses during this book for you to quickly put play into practice. Such play breaks will help you to make sense of what we are talking about in an experiential way. But play is a practice – it is about doing and it is not intended to be over-scripted or directed, so I invite you to engage with the play in this book as *an invitation* to embrace a more playful state of mind.

I am a psychotherapist and I do a lot of specialised work in attachment repair, trauma recovery, and strengthening and enhancing the parent–child relationship through play. I am passionate about play. I would even say that I have been in pursuit of play for most of my career, dedicated to finding ways to ensure that we all live more playful lives and approach life with a more playful state of mind.

I asked the following questions on my social media about play and adulthood:

- Do you believe that you are a playful person? 49% answered yes.
- Do you make time in your week for playfulness (e.g. via weekly activities/a class)? 81% said no.
- Do you believe that you have enough time and opportunity for play in your life? 84% said no.
- Would you like some practical ways to become more playful in your life? 89% said yes.
- Do you believe that playfulness improves your relationships with other adults in your life? 93% said yes.
- Do you believe that playfulness impacts our mental health? 92% said yes.

People who follow me on social media are, most likely, already interested in the play content I post and are already somewhat invested in becoming a more playful person. So if this group of people is struggling to find or make time in their adult lives to become more playful, in spite of really wanting to and almost half already feeling that they are playful, what is missing?

One respondent talked about how their desire to embrace play more in their adult lives was affected by their fear that other adults, specifically work colleagues, would not take them seriously and would deem them 'silly'. Another said that they would feel too self-conscious to just play for their own benefit (they said they were happy to play with children but not alone or with other adults); however, this person also added that they had *really* enjoyed the freedom of jumping when they took a turn on the family trampoline. I also asked if people remembered their favourite play activity from childhood (72% said yes), if they still played that game now in adulthood (11% yes) and if they could play it now, would they (62% yes). Another spoke of the joy they experienced when both adults and children all joined together in a game of hide and seek at a family gathering.

Someone else who is an artist spoke of how they don't really consciously schedule in play via such things as weekly classes, reflecting that play was very much integrated into their way of living due to holding a creative attitude towards most things. This person added that the scheduled play (a class) is a treat for them and something they only do once in a while.

Overall, self-consciousness and a lack of time were preventing most people from getting the level of play they wished they could have in their lives. When the opportunities to play arose, they were enjoyed. This tells me that most of us will benefit from *prescribed playtime* each day to get us going.

While there is a wealth of research into the importance and impact of play in the lives of children, there is relatively little into its relevance in the lives of adults. Perhaps this is because we tend, particularly in Western society, to view play as belonging only in childhood. The adult world conditions us to place *seriousness* above *playfulness*. The problem with this is that it entirely misses the point! Play *is* a serious business, with serious impact on our lives.

What the research does show us is that play (across our lifespan, including our adult lives) establishes safe and secure relationships and is central to building trust and a strong emotional connection between people while reducing incidents of relational conflict and improving communication.

Play and playfulness are all around us. Without play we wouldn't have art, music, dance, poetry. Just think what a joyless world that would be! Play is central to the human experience, and just as we change and develop as we grow older, how we play needs to change and grow with us.

This book is dedicated to the role of play in the lives of adults. Not for parents per se, and certainly not *only* for parents, but for all of us adults because we will all benefit from creating opportunities for increased playfulness in our lives.

I will start with exploring *the science of play* and specifically what the social, emotional and even physical health benefits there are for us in embracing a more playful state of mind. Then I will delve into the darker side of play and how a playful adulthood can help heal inherited trauma from childhood, and how we experienced being parented. I will explore how we can change the stories we live by – the inherited family narrative that shapes and informs how we live our lives. After this, I will examine the role of playfulness in all our relationships – from the parent–child dynamic, to friendships, to intimate partner relationships and broader family relationships. And I will end with exploring how a playful state of mind makes us perform better in our professional work because play fuels the kind of flexibility and adaptability that strengthens and enhances our creativity and productivity.

This book is an invitation and roadmap to a more playful state of mind so that we can nurture our own capacity for empathy and creativity. We will take a journey to explore why this matters so much and why play might well be the small change that will make a big difference in how you live your life.

We need space and time to be mindfully present and play-fully engaged each day. By creating this dedicated time and space, we create opportunities for moments-of-meeting – for connection and for shared joy. When we feel that we are enjoyed by others in our lives, we experience a deeper sense of joy within ourselves.

What comes to mind when you read the phrase 'create space and take time for yourself'? There is no right or wrong answer to this, I am simply curious as to what picture these words paint in your mind. Close your eyes now and repeat to yourself, *I am creating space and taking time for myself.* Where do you see yourself? What are you doing? Are you alone or with someone, and if you are with someone, who is it? How are you feeling in this moment? And remember that all feelings are valid so if this stirs up some anxiety within you at this point, permit that, acknowledge that feeling.

When I do this, I see myself on holiday, somewhere quiet and bright, sunny but not too hot, with things to do and see but not too much distraction either. My kind of holiday. Yours will be different and that is how it should be. A holiday is supposed to give us all a break from our norm and our day-to-day lives. It's an opportunity to reflect on what is and is not working well for us in terms of how we are living our lives. A holiday is a change of environment, a chance to change our field of vision and rest our busy task-oriented brains as we emotionally exhale and recharge our batteries. If we over-schedule or seek to 'prescribe fun' on a holiday, we sabotage the opportunity for all of this. I invite you to approach this book in a holiday state of mind.

Our busy lives can leave us very time poor and, in my work, I all too often see that play is the first thing to be sacrificed. We are often running from one urgent task to another and feel we don't have time to be playful. It isn't a priority because we have forgotten its value in our lives. This is a shame because taking and asking for time to play is precisely how we see what is and isn't working in our routines and schedules, and in our lives.

We have never needed play in our lives more than now. Can we emerge from the Covid-19 pandemic in a more playful state of mind, and what might that mean for us both culturally and societally? What does it mean in our lives as adults and parents? What role does play have in corporate culture in a post-pandemic world? Can we move from an *all work and no play* attitude to a more *productive work depends on time to play* attitude?

Throughout this book, we will explore together how we are all surrounded by opportunities for and invitations to embrace play in our world, especially through language (sounds, songs, poems) and culture (here, I am defining culture as *how we do things*). You do not need to come to this book as a creative person, although at its core, this book is a story of how we all have the capacity to live more creative lives.

Now, let's get playful, starting with this play reflective exercise to bring us into connection with how we currently understand play and its role in our lives.

PLAY BREAK

Play reflection exercise

- Do you believe that you have a playful side?
- When did you last feel playful?

- Who brings out your playful side?
- What kind of activities feel like play to you?
- What kind of activities add energy to how you feel and behave?
- What kind of activities help you feel calm and soothed?
- Where in your life are you your most playful?
- Who in your life are you most playful with?
- Are you happy with your current level of playfulness?
- Are you open to creating space for more playfulness in your life?
- What difference will this make in your life?

Take a moment to sit with your answers from this reflective exercise. Are there any surprises for you in your answers? Are you content with what these answers tell you? Are there any you would like to change?

Sometimes, reflective exercises can confront us with an uncomfortable truth. If you are disappointed with some of your answers here or perhaps how your life does not currently include space for more playfulness, I invite you to consider it as an opportunity for change.

UNSTICKING OURSELVES FROM FEELING STUCK

When we reflect on the lack of playfulness in our lives or feel overwhelmed by the busyness of our life so that we feel we have no room for anything else, not even play, it can immobilise us.

Have you ever felt blocked or stuck within yourself or within your life, even one area of your life? I'm sure you have because at one point or another, who among us hasn't experienced this life fatigue, this stuckness? I believe that when we experience this blocked or stuck feeling within ourselves or our lives, it is an acknowledgement that we have forgotten our need to play. This is because play fuels flexibility and adaptability. The capacity to be flexible and adaptable is an essential life skill that enables us to bend without breaking when the landscape around us shifts.

The Covid-19 pandemic really brought this home for me. With no notice we were called on to draw from the depths of our flexibility and adaptability. But think back to how you passed this time, particularly the first lockdown period when there was an air of novelty and this too shall (soon) pass about it all. Were you baking banana bread in more ways than you previously knew existed? Were you growing your own sourdough starter? Did you teach yourself the piano via YouTube tutorials or take up cross-stitch or knitting? Perhaps you splurged on the 'Starship Enterprise' of home coffee machines and are now a self-taught amateur barista. What are any of these things if not playing?

Play makes us more flexible and adaptable certainly, but what emerges from that flexibility? We get to wonder how things might look and feel if we were to approach the situation in a new or different way. This shift in thinking opens a door to possibility, and when we feel that anything is possible, we enjoy a surge in hopefulness, which in turn strengthens and enhances our capacity for positive mental health and well-being.

Let's take a brief pause here and try this out in a playful activity.

What if?: You do not need any props for this one. Just an open mind and a smidge of imagination.

- What would happen if... the sky turned green and the grass turned blue?
- What would happen if... we started our lives as adults and aged backwards?
- What would happen if... humans had no noses?
- What would happen if... humans barked and dogs talked?
- What would happen if... we all lived our lives as a constant musical?

Pick one from this list and wonder it out to a conclusion. Then go back and take another one and repeat the exercise.

See if doing this a couple of times makes you wonder about your own scenario and go with that. This list is intended to get you going – wondering is limitless. You can be as silly/ frivolous or as serious as you want with this – so long as you are wondering, you are playing.

We need to challenge our preconceived notions of what play is and is not and how it might look and feel for each of us. Play is not a box of toys in the corner of a room. It is a state of mind and a way of being. When we are faced with a challenge in our lives and can bring ourselves to a starting point of *I wonder if...*, we are approaching the matter from a playful state of mind. In this way, 'I wonder' can be viewed as an indispensable life skill. As you read this book, please do so in this state of wondering. Wonder if this book can offer you fresh thinking and a new (or renewed) perspective on how you live and connect with others in your life.

CHAPTER ONE

The Science of Play: Why It's Good for Us

When I say that play is a state of mind, I am describing play as a neural exercise. Play can help us to up- and down-regulate our emotional arousal as required. It can serve as a brake to slow us down and as an accelerator to speed us up when we feel sluggish and flat. Knowing how to tune into our arousal state and how to slow it down or speed it up, depending on what is needed, is what makes us more flexible and adaptable in the face of life's challenges. This capacity helps to prevent us getting stuck in a heightened anxious state where it can feel hard to switch off and also help prevent us zoning out or switching off for lengthy periods. In essence, this means that play and playfulness serve to keep us regulated and out of survival mode, which can deplete us physically and emotionally. In a playful state of mind, we can enjoy the activation of play without getting hyper-aroused or hypo-aroused. This is about keeping our internal system in check – at least mostly in check, most of the time.

Just as we exercise our physical muscles to keep us healthy, strong and physically flexible, we also need to work on our play muscles so that our playful side is healthy and strong enough to fuel the flexibility we rely on in negotiating life's ups and downs. This investment in play also serves to strengthen a healthy nervous system, making it more flexible, stronger and more regulated. This means that we can tolerate a surge in energy entering our nervous system when we need to react and respond to a challenge in our lives without that surge activating our fight/flight/freeze response system. Thus, we are flexible and adaptable to stressful experiences and can react and respond appropriately without getting overwhelmed by those experiences.

When we are aroused by our fight/flight/freeze impulses, it is very difficult to feel or act in a creative and playful way. This makes it hard for us to consider the perspectives of others, to manage our impulses and to make healthy life choices. This also means that our nervous system is sensitised and can be very easily activated, leaving us feeling physically and emotionally exhausted and depleted. There is always a reason as to why our nervous system became activated in this way – often repeated, distressing and even traumatic experiences from our past have rendered us highly sensitive and primed to react all of the time. But by choosing to consciously shift towards a more playful way of living, we can strengthen and enhance our capacity for self-regulation and thereby map new ways for our nervous system to read, interpret and respond to experiences that serve us better. Through play, we are resourcing our autonomic nervous system to become more resilient; we can regulate the stress that life throws our way and can respond to the demands and challenges we encounter through life.

POLYVAGAL THEORY – THE SCIENCE OF SAFETY

Our autonomic nervous system is a complex internal system that essentially takes care of our body's basic housekeeping. These are the things that happen internally without us being consciously aware of them, such as remembering to breathe, our heart beating, and digesting food. Best described as the science of safety, polyvagal theory[1] helps us to understand how our autonomic nervous system is shaped and how we travel it

---

1   Polyvagal theory was developed by Dr Stephen Porges, a
    scientist and researcher, and his colleague Deb Dana, who
    took his research and found ways to make it accessible
    and applicable to how we live our day-to-day lives.
    Because of the work of Porges and Dana, we have a greater
    understanding of how the regulation and dysregulation
    of these polyvagal pathways seek to either communicate
    or conceal what is happening inside our bodies to other
    people. I have recommended the work of Dr Stephen
    Porges and Deb Dana in the resources at the back of this
    book should you want to find out more about this.

via pathways of protection (when we are dysregulated, disconnected, under stress or trauma) or pathways of connection
(when we feel safe, regulated and connected both internally
and externally with others and within the world around us).
Polyvagal theory identifies a specific type of nervous system
arousal – our social engagement system – which describes a
playful blend of activating and calming states of arousal. This
is the system that helps us to negotiate and connect within
relationships with others and enables us to become more
flexible and adaptable to stressful experiences in our lives.

We are always scanning our environments for signs of
threat/safety. Some studies show we do it as often as every
fifth of a second and that this scanning is happening at an
unconscious level. Sounds like a lot but for most of us, at least
most of the time, this provides us with a reassuring loop that
we are safe, we are safe, we are still safe. This helps us to feel
grounded and safe, both internally and externally.

But some of us may have grown up without that reassuring loop, in an unsafe or unpredictable environment. In this
instance, perhaps our safety sensor got stuck on high alert
and our autonomic nervous system was saturated in stress
hormones. Heightened levels of cortisol told us we were under
threat, turning us into emotional meerkats, heightening our
level of anticipatory arousal and making us emotionally scan
around for who or what was going to kick off any moment

now. We were primed to react. We would either fight, flee, freeze or fawn. People sometimes assume we have either a fight or flight impulse and that is it, but in truth we have more complex adaptive strategies depending on the level of stress or trauma we have grown up with, who perpetrated that trauma, the duration and frequency of the event and the presence or absence of people who made us feel safe in our lives.

Imagine yourself walking through a forest. Look around, note what you see, hear, smell and how you feel. Suddenly, you see a bear. It is a large, angry, threatening bear. It rises up on its hind legs, primed to attack you. How do you feel? What goes through your mind? What is happening in your body? How is your breathing, your heart rate? Where are you looking right now? What are you going to do? Some of us will be primed to stick up our fists and fight the bear; some of us will be primed to turn on our heels and run as fast as we can away from the bear. Others will be primed to assess the situation quickly and decide that freezing, staying as quiet and as still as possible is the best response in the hope that the bear doesn't notice us and moves on past us. Others again may feel like the way to stay safe is to become like the bear, change behaviour, appearance and communication to become as bear-like as possible in a bid to 'befriend' and soothe the bear.

No one of these reactions is right or wrong or better or worse than the others. We do not have conscious control over how we react. That is hardwired into us based on our earliest experiences of being cared for and is influenced by the experiences we have had throughout our lives. And of course, however we reacted to the above will have made sense and served us as well as possible when it was a bear in the forest. Consider how this would affect you if you lived with the bear. If the bear came home every night and you always needed to stay primed to react, to keep yourself safe from the bear. Quite quickly, you would see that the strategies that feel adaptive and life-saving in the forest with the bear become maladaptive and life-limiting when they are a chronic and repeated experience.

Polyvagal theory links the mechanisms underlying feelings of safety, social interaction and healthy development. But more than this, through polyvagal theory we learn that recovery is always possible. We can shift from pathways of protection to pathways of connection by learning ways to change our more unhealthy default mechanisms to healthier strategies.

In polyvagal theory, we talk about *neuroception*. This is different from how we understand perception because with neuroception it is what we pick up on at a body level; it can be an unconscious detection but we respond to it nonetheless. Think of neuroception as your internal surveillance system. Perhaps we respond by getting irritable, avoidant or aggressive, or maybe we respond by getting tired, lethargic and shutting down.

UNDERSTANDING YOUR VAGAL NERVES

There are three vagal nerves, called *ventral vagus, sympathetic vagus* and *dorsal vagus*. These three nerves run from our brain to the lower gut, travelling through our facial muscles, heart, lungs and gut.

The ventral vagus is where we feel safe and regulated. Let's call this one 'home'. This is where we want to stay most of the time, pitch our tent or throw down our anchor. But we all have a home away from home, that place we go to when we do not feel safe and regulated. For some of us this will be the *sympathetic vagus*, a place of activation and mobilisation, and for some of us it will be the *dorsal vagus*, which is a place of low energy and shutting down where we feel we are just going through the motions but not really present.

For me, I know that my home away from home is sympathetic arousal. When I am stressed or emotionally dysregulated, I tend to do more, take on more, go, go, go at an almost frenetic pace. I respond by getting as busy and preoccupied as possible. Because I know that I do this, I have (over the years, as it took a long time for me to really understand this about myself and to see it as a challenge not a strength) developed conscious strategies that pull me towards more dorsal-paced introspection as my route back to that ventral place of safety and regulation. I do a monthly somatic massage. I practice yoga weekly. I make time to read, which for me is a great way to quieten my brain and escape whatever else is going on.

If you default to a dorsal retreat in times of stress and dysregulation, it might look like climbing under the duvet, pulling a weighted blanket over yourself, pulling down the blackout blinds, turning the phone off and shutting the world out. In this type of shutdown, you will need conscious strategies to mobilise yourself upwards. Make yourself get up and shower or go for a walk or eat something. Start slowly and build up your activation level (perhaps turn on your favourite song and dance) until you are back in your ventral space of safety and regulation.

It is healthy for our nervous system to move up and down during the day. While we are at our optimum level of arousal within the safe bandwidth of our window of tolerance (where things will feel safe and comfortable for us), we are also designed to move outside that window of tolerance when we perceive threat in our autonomic nervous systems. We all need to be able to travel these vagal pathways to stay safe, healthy and regulated. We cannot totally eliminate stress, and we are all prone to times of dysregulation as we respond and react to unpredictable life events, so, instead, we need to focus on how we can recognise, read and respond to our levels of dysregulation.

When our nervous system becomes chronically dysregu-lated, we are stuck outside the window of tolerance – either hyper-aroused (elevated, frenetic, unable to switch off) or hypo-aroused (zoned out, switched off, no motivation, apathetic). We experience an emotional flooding to our system and cannot recover that place of safety and regulation within ourselves, so we get 'stuck'. This may cause us to seek out unhealthy habits in an attempt to regulate our dysfunctional nervous system (unhealthy levels of food, alcohol, self-injurious behaviours, dangerous situations). While these might well provide some temporary relief, it is an artificial relief, and they will not afford us access to authentic regulation and safety, without which we cannot experience comfort and calm because we are sitting in a simmering state of agitation and internal discomfort.

Consider this example:

Sarah has just finished a ten-hour working day. It is her third such day in a row this week and it is only Thursday. She is tired and thinks about a hot bath and an early night. In her bag, her phone vibrates. Once, twice, three times in a row. Without looking, Sarah knows that these are emails with more work from her manager, all of which will be flagged as urgent. She doesn't want to look at her phone; she had promised herself she wouldn't work into her evening at home again tonight. Her phone vibrates again. That's a fourth message. She starts to tap her leg and wring her fingers on her lap. She feels a knot in her stomach. She reaches for her phone, but just to look at social media she

*tells herself as the number of unread emails steadily rises
on the app on her home screen.*

Trigger (that pushes her outside of her window of tolerance
and activates her nervous system) = emails with (perceived)
demand from her manager that she addresses immediately.

Hyper-aroused state (spike in anxiety, difficulty switching
off) = thoughts start filling in the blanks with assumptions
and judgements as to how her manager will perceive her if she
doesn't answer, with physiological responses such as tapping
leg and wringing fingers.

Artificial window of tolerance (this doesn't help and only
serves to prolong the stress) = believes she can use the phone
that is triggering her to self-regulate by ignoring emails and
scrolling social media.

What could Sarah do to help her return to her true window
of tolerance?

- Set her email to give an out-of-office response outside
  designated work hours.

- Ask to meet with her manager to agree some boundaries around work communication.
- Take the email app off her phone or disable it outside work hours.
- Call a friend to chat and laugh with on her way home.
- Consider that her manager likes to work different hours and that she doesn't have to respond to these emails and she should take her bath and have her early night as planned.

I use this example as I think it is quite a common one that many of us will relate to.

A playful mind would help Sarah to:

- be curious as to what might be motivating her manager to send work communication outside designated work hours
- wonder about what is and is not expected of her
- pursue her own connections to self-regulate after such long demanding work hours
- recognise her own needs and respond to what her mind and body requires in the moment
- establish and maintain boundaries.

Playfulness wouldn't stop Sarah feeling triggered in the situation but would serve her well in identifying that she is being triggered and equip her with alternative actions and solutions in the moment. She would be better able to downregulate and take a more holistic view of the situation. Our nervous system can (re)learn tools of regulation. Recognising we are dysregulated and have a route to the restoration of regulation is precisely how we become resilient.

Play fuels connection and so reduces our cues of danger while actively increasing our cues of safety. The physically active but interpersonal nature of face-to-face playfulness with others can be especially useful in combining cues of safety while upregulating the state of emotional arousal. This increases the scope of feeling safe in physical proximity to others and thus the scope of arousal that can be tolerated without us falling into one of those fight/flight/freeze/fawn states.

Play and playfulness are a lovely combination of ventral safety and regulation, with the activation and mobilisation of sympathetic energy. All is good when these two states blend in a playful and harmonious way, but when they get out of synch, the sympathetic mobilising energy takes over and something like rough-and-tumble play becomes too rough. The fun play becomes aggressive and laughter quickly becomes tears. We have all seen this with children, and a lot of us will have experienced this as children. But let's also consider how this can happen in our adult lives. Consider how players in a team sport can escalate into an aggressive situation of 'foul play'. Consider how a family board game can escalate into a row, with accusations of cheating.

Recognising these tendencies in ourselves is part of the challenge, but developing strategies that enable us to recover regulation is the other very important part.

THE BENEFITS OF MICRO MOMENTS OF JOY

Micro moments of joy can help us stay rooted in that safe and regulated ventral vagus and are especially useful at times of uncertainty, stress and dysregulation.

How can we practise these daily micro moments in our adult lives? Try this polyvagal exercise.

Track your glimmers and convert them to a glow[2]: A glimmer is a micro moment of joy that is around us every day, something that we frequently overlook as not being important. These micro moments are tiny sparks of joy that help to anchor us in that safe and regulated ventral home. Start your practice by looking for what might be more predictable glimmers for you, things you already include in your daily routines that you enjoy doing. For example:

---

2   Dana, D. (2018). *The Polyvagal Theory in Therapy*. New York: Norton & Co. (p.68).

- That first sip of ice-cold orange juice/smell of freshly brewed coffee.
- The feeling when you arrive at the bus stop or train platform just as your bus or train pulls up.
- The feeling of warmth on your face or a cool breeze blowing through your hair.
- Opening the biscuit tin at work and finding your favourite biscuit is still there.
- Making eye contact with someone and smiling at each other at the same time.

A glimmer is a small, everyday moment of joy. Something that sparks positive energy, even fleetingly.

Where possible, share your glimmers with someone in your life, someone who understands what they are and perhaps is joining you in the daily practice. If you'd rather not involve someone else, you can record your glimmers in a notebook and this will serve as a daily record and reminder of the joy in your life.

Set an intention to look for a certain number of glimmers each day. I suggest that you choose an attainable number and start in a modest way as you can always build up or surpass your goal, which is better than saying you will track ten per day and feeling that you have failed. So, let's say that you will start with three glimmers per day and will review your daily goal and adjust accordingly.

To take this exercise a step further, you can work on converting your glimmers to a glow. I suggest you focus on tracking your daily glimmers for a period of a month or until it feels like an automatic impulse you have developed before you build on the practice to ensure you get the most benefit from it.

To convert a glimmer to a glow, you must savour it. Savouring is when you hold the glimmer moment for 30–60 seconds, soaking up the positive emotional resonance it affords you. Taking my list above, let's work on how we might savour each of those glimmers:

- That first sip of ice-cold orange juice – stay in the moment as you feel its coldness run down your throat towards your stomach.

- The first smell of freshly brewed coffee – hold the cup in between your two hands and feel its warmth on your skin, deeply inhale the smell and hold that while you take the first sip and taste the coffee (or tea or hot chocolate).

- The feeling when you arrive at the bus stop or train platform just as your bus or train pulls up – smile broadly, say aloud (or to yourself but aloud means you hear your own words and share it with someone else who may reflect the moment back to you), 'Oh I love it when that happens.'

- Opening the biscuit tin at work and finding your favourite biscuit is still there – take the biscuit, enjoy the biscuit and for the minute or so it takes to eat that biscuit, be only focused on it.

- Making eye contact with someone and smiling at each other at the same time – add a word, say hello if it is a stranger, and if it is someone you know, add a physical connection such as a hug, handshake or high five to deepen and extend the connection of the moment.

With a glimmer, you pause just long enough to acknowledge that a spark of joy is happening, and with a glow you are holding on to that acknowledgement long enough to embed the moment into your autonomic nervous system, maximising the benefits for you, which includes feeling calmer yet also more energetic, along with an improved positive outlook.

PLAY BUILDS EMOTIONAL RESILIENCE

Embracing opportunities for play and investing in a more playful life is a practical, accessible and effective way of investing in resources and helps us to build our capacity for emotional resilience. Resilience is something that is often misrepresented in terms of you either have it or don't. The idea that some of us simply are resilient and some of us are not is inaccurate. Resilience is not an automatic default setting that any of us just have, be we adults or children.

Resilience can only emerge when our stressors do not outweigh our resources to cope. Resilience is about managing this balance, and this is an active and ongoing process. Very few people are resilient all of the time because we build resilience by moving through cycles of feeling regulated, dysregulated and then experiencing the restoration of regulation. It is akin to a dance. We are in synch, out of synch and getting back into synch. Resilience is not simply something that we are, it is something that we develop over the course of our lives and in response to the life events we experience. Resilience increases our capacity for flexibility in terms of how we respond to such life events. It is feeling tethered even when walking on shifting sands. It is also something that is teachable and learnable though this process takes time, practice, patience and persistent awareness. And it matters because resilience keeps us hopeful when things around us might feel hopeless.

The rhythm of synchrony that resilience depends on is very similar to the rhythm of synchrony that play establishes. Being in synch, out of synch and getting back into synch is like the harmony described earlier in this chapter when the safe, regulated ventral vagal energy blends with the activating, mobilising energy of sympathetic arousal. They are harmonious when in synch with each other (fun and laughter), but when the sympathetic arousal takes over, they are out of synch (laughter becomes tears) and generally there is a process of repair (saying sorry, seeking comfort to co-regulate before returning to play with renewed optimism and hope).

Resilience is teachable, but learning how to move towards greater levels of resilience takes time, practice, patience and persistent effort... and it takes play!

THE IMPORTANCE OF PLAY IN BUILDING RESILIENCE

But we must give ourselves permission to play and that goes hand in hand with giving ourselves permission to feel exactly how we feel. It may sound a bit ridiculous that we would need permission to feel, but when you think about it, we are conditioned to suppress true feelings in favour of overt politeness and to avoid *causing a fuss* from a very young age. When we suppress our authentic emotions, we can become quite unaware of our feelings, resulting in us growing up into emotionally under-skilled adults. But we can reclaim emotional fluency through the creative medium of play.

Authentic feelings are messy, chaotic and don't always come out as we intended them to but are an overt expression of who and, moreover, *how* we are. Our feelings are continuously present, changing and evolving throughout our day and we are never not in a state of some kind of emotion. To not feel would mean not living. And this is not something to take lightly.

We need to reclaim emotional fluency *so that* we can live happy, healthy and fulfilled lives. So ask yourself: *How am I feeling?* Right now, in this very moment, just pause and acknowledge how you are truly feeling. Once you have it, wonder why it is you are feeling this way. What is the story of this feeling state in this moment – what happened today that has resulted in your feeling this way? What does feeling this way make you want to do?

Let me share a personal example of this with you. Today I was feeling frustrated and quite stressed out. I had a lot of work demands on me and felt I was short on time for everything. The more worked up I got, the less productive I became. I turned to look out of my office window (something I do when my brain feels overwhelmed as I believe that changing our field of vision can help reset a busy, frazzled brain) and I saw that it was raining heavily. I watched and listened to the rain for a minute and felt my breathing slow down. And as I calmed, I had an idea, a notion perhaps. I got up, went downstairs, put on my wellies and went outside and jumped in some puddles. I jumped softly at first, then more and more vigorously. I spent five minutes splashing through puddles outside and the pure playful joy of it revived me, utterly restored me and enabled me to complete a productive afternoon's work in a way a cup of tea and sighing at my laptop just wasn't going to.

Emotions are an important source of information in our lives. Acknowledging our true and authentic emotions allows us to capture what is happening within us in response to the world (and people) outside us. Once upon a time, it may have been asserted that emotions got in the way of productivity and getting things done, but this just isn't the case: emotions and awareness of our emotions *is* how we get things done. Emotions drive our creativity and productivity, and play drives our emotions. A little burst of play in my afternoon helped to shift me from frustrated stuckness to joyful creativity. Sometimes, the answer really is that simple. Play unlocks our suppressed emotions, it unsticks us when we are emotionally stuck and it shows us that there is *always* another way of thinking, feeling, approaching and doing something. Play is a resource in our lives that helps to build and sustain our resilience to cope with challenges.

Something I often speak of is that play is a language and moreover it is the language of children. Language is, in and of itself, a play space. We are born into a sea of language, sounds, phonemes, all of which provide a sensuous experience for the mouth as we play with language acquisition. Mmm mmm becomes Mama, apf becomes apple, and so on. Phonemes are a great way to consider this. A phoneme is a sound that makes sense. Take for example, *uh-oh* or *ouch* or *oo-er*. When you hear these sounds, you know immediately what is being conveyed. Say them aloud now and repeat them in different tones of voice. Note how the prosody (the musicality, the pitch, pace, tone) of your voice changes the meaning conveyed by the sound in subtle but significant ways. What other phonemes can you add in? This is when sound dominates over sense. The constancy and consistency of sound is central to language acquisition and it is something that adults freely engage in with fluidity and fluency when 'talking' to young babies/children. We are rhythmic creatures; the voice *is* music, and sometimes it is discordant and sometimes it is harmonic.

Far beyond the acquisition of speech, this playfulness with language returns later in our lives in the guise of poetry and song. Rhythm and synchrony trigger the sub-systems of the brain associated with emotional regulation so it stands to reason that we feel called by this form of playfulness and that we can feel restored, calmed and (re)invigorated by it.

MISTAKES ARE WHERE THE MAGIC HAPPENS

In this book, I am sharing play activities that can be engaged with as a solo endeavour (and later on some more that are about partner play and mutual play). This is because I want us to take a journey starting with ourselves and giving ourselves permission to fumble with play as we get back in touch with the part of us that recognises the rhythm and synchrony that work for us. There is no right way to play because play has an incongruous relationship with perfection. Perfection stifles the process of play because it eliminates curiosity and there is no play without curiosity.

You do not need to possess a fully stocked craft room or expensive art materials or a top-of-the-range camera, or hold mastery of a musical instrument, or gain credentials to equip you to play. And really, stockpiling such supplies will get in the way of you playing because you will simply feel you do not have the right equipment, need to wait until you do and that the equipment you have invested in should be used in a particular way… sabotaging creativity with rules (I will talk about the function of rules in play later on).

My daughter has a book called *Beautiful Oops!* by Barney Saltzberg that I was looking at recently and it reminded me again of how important mistakes are to both creativity and play. It is a book that celebrates our mistakes. We are all living in a world that is increasingly unforgiving of mistakes. Social media can be a very shaming space in this regard, but if we stop embracing mistakes as opportunities to grow and learn, opportunities to create something new, we are missing the point entirely. This book takes the everyday 'mistakes' any of us make, such as spilling a drink, tearing a page while turning it, making a deep page fold when we close a book, and transforms them into something beautiful. Every smudge and stain and tear is an idea and an opportunity to create. I just love it, and while it is written for children, it is actually a great reminder to adults of all there is to be learned and celebrated in mistakes. The next time you smudge, stain or tear something, instead of getting frustrated or throwing it away, pause and play with it for a few minutes. There is a certain magic in mistakes, if we are not so fearful of them and focused on defending them that we can pause and creatively use them.

Freud wrote about what he called the psychopathologies of everyday life. These are the bungled actions of our lives, the things we drop, the train of thought we lose, the forgetfulness, the mess and chaos of everyday life – the mistakes we make. He saw it as the many ways that our unconscious mind expresses itself in these 'slips' and errors we make. We all do silly things, make what we may dismiss and minimise as 'stupid mistakes', but perhaps our creativity and capacity for imagination would be strengthened and enhanced if instead of dismissing these mistakes, we stopped and listened to them.

What if we celebrated the joy of a bungled action, laughed at our own silliness and expressed curiosity about the things that we forget? What could we create out of the clumsiness of everyday life? This would be about looking for the learning in our mistakes, celebrating mistakes as expressions of inner chaos from which something new could emerge – a new idea, a fresh perspective, a moment of meeting and connection when we acknowledge our mistake and apologise for it. But sadly, growing up can render us avoidant of imaginative leaps, resulting in us staying stuck in the now, even if we are frustrated and feel restricted in how we are living, rather than imagine another way, another future for ourselves because that feels like a leap of imagination into an unknown, uncertain space.

PLAY BREAK

Scribble art

Here is one I tend to do when I am feeling frustrated, fed up or stuck with a task that I am grappling with. It takes anywhere from 5 to 15 minutes and when I play in this way, I find that I emerge from it in a more creative state of mind that enables me to return to the previous task with a different kind of energy and focus.

Here is an example of one I did with the scribble done on the left and what I created from it on the right:

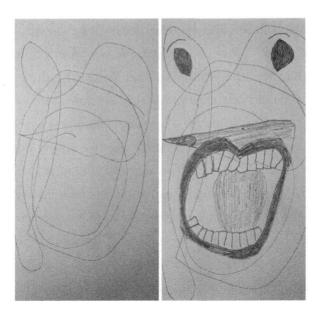

Try it yourself. You will need: a sheet of blank paper and a pen/pencil.

Place the sheet of paper in a landscape position on a flat surface in front of you. Pick up the pencil in your non-dominant hand. Put the point of the pencil anywhere on the page in front of you. Now close your eyes and as you count to 15 slowly in your head, just scribble around the page, without peeking. Once you get to 15, open your eyes and turn the page 180 degrees to the right (flip it around in other words). Now, using the pencil in your usual writing/dominant hand, turn your scribble into something. Anything at all. Add facial features, aspects of nature, people, animals, shapes, whatever comes to mind. When done, sit back and look at what you have created. Give your piece a name that you feel best describes it and how you feel looking at it.

Take 2: Try it another way. You will need: a sheet of paper and a pen/pencil.

Place the sheet of paper on a surface in front of you. Close your eyes and picture a place that you visited often as a child. It should be a place that you experienced joy in. Now bring to mind one specific time you went there. Who were you with, what happened, how did it feel? Try to bring to mind as many details as you can. What you saw, smelled, tasted, felt and thought. Holding that in mind, pick up your pencil in your non-dominant hand and place it somewhere on the page (your eyes are still closed and should remain closed until the end of this activity). Draw the place you are thinking of in as much detail as you can in accordance with what has returned to your mind. When you feel finished, take a deep breath in and slowly exhale. Open your eyes and look at your drawing in front of you. Look at the shapes, the size, the representation.

There are lots of theories about non-dominant hand drawing but the reason I encourage it is that it can serve to by-pass our internal critic or that feeling that we are not good at drawing. I also believe that it can help to move beyond that logical, conscious part of our brain and bring us deeper to our unconscious in that we draw what we see in our mind and feel when we recall something rather than what we 'know' it to look like. I have further invited you to close your eyes to ensure your focus isn't on accuracy but on the memory as you recall/picture it in your mind.

THE JOY OF A JOYFUL MINDSET

As I mentioned in the introduction, we tend to relegate play to the realm of childhood, which does it a great disservice. Our need for play doesn't end in childhood. It changes in rhythm and content as we grow, but we rely on playfulness in our lives to shape and develop our brain and bodies even as adults.

The message I really want to convey in this book is that we *all* have a capacity for playfulness, and it is something that we can nurture and (re)grow in our lives. If you have ever spent time observing children at play, you might have experienced a spark of joy in doing so. Observing play can remind us of simpler times when life was about fun and enjoyment, so just imagine what time spent playing can affect for us. Play sparks joy for us individually but also within relationships.

We tend to use the terms joy and happiness interchangeably but they are not the same. Happiness is an outward expression; it is an emotional response to someone or a situation. Joy is an inner feeling; it comes from within you not outside you. Joy endures regardless of circumstance. We can choose joy and we can nurture and develop it from within us. Joy sustains us through hardships and enables us to connect with ourselves, others and the outside world with meaning. Joy is less transitory than happiness and is not dependent on external circumstances. So, invest in joy, aim to enjoy and allow yourself to be enjoyed.

I often speak about the importance of having joy in our lives. Jaak Panksepp, an Estonian-American neuroscientist and psychobiologist, was a researcher into the genetics of play, and in his research, he discovered that social joy changes the brain in important ways. He also researched the neural effects of laughter and play in stimulating social joy and how this affected the brain in ways that could counteract psychological pain or distress. Dr Stuart Brown is a psychiatrist and founder of the National Institute for Play in California. He describes play in adults as being as unique to the individual adult as their fingerprint, but what all play experiences have in common is engagement and pleasure. He advocates that play is a basic human need and when we are low on playfulness, our minds and bodies notice, making us more rigid, grumpy and pessimistic. But for play to effect a meaningful change to our well-being, it must be something we practise regularly rather than saving up for our two-week annual holiday.

Research into the physical and relational benefits of happiness/joy is increasing. In 2011, the United Nations (which produces an annual World Happiness Report) issued a resolution stipulating that the pursuit of happiness is a fundamental human goal and that its member states should undertake practical actions to link the measurement of social and economic development with the happiness and well-being of its citizens. Also, Meik Wiking, the Danish author of books on *hygge* (comfort) and *lykke* (happiness) and CEO of the Happiness Research Institute, a think tank in Copenhagen, has explored the causes and effects of human happiness with the goal of working towards a better quality of life for all global citizens.

Joy isn't just something nice to have in our lives, it truly is an essential component to staying well, both physically and mentally.

However, joy doesn't just come to us. It is grown and it is nurtured in us, ideally from early childhood. In order to enjoy life, to enjoy others, we have to have experienced being enjoyed by others. Shared joy is the route to a joyous life. One of the most powerful influences on your nervous system is the people you surround yourself with. This influence will either serve to nourish or deplete you. We all need healthy, joyful connections in our lives. Without them we will struggle to stay in a safe and regulated space within our nervous system and will feel pulled into a defensive (sympathetic) stance or withdraw into shutdown and disconnection (dorsal). Not everyone in your life will spark joy, and no one will spark pure joy all of the time because this is real life and not a musical. But try to ensure that you have more people who do spark joy in your life than those who deplete your resources. We need supportive social connections to flourish.

The connection you had with your parents/caregivers as a child shaped you, your brain and your nervous system, and determined your capacity to self-regulate. The effects of this early formation will echo throughout your life, impacting on the connections you form and your capacity to manage stress.

Reflect on how you were responded to in times of distress and struggle as a child. How did that make you feel then and how does it make you feel now to recall it? How do you wish you had been responded to and how would that have made a difference? Can you give that kind of desired response to yourself now as an adult?

TRACK YOUR JOY

In your play reflection exercise in the introduction to this book, you answered the question, 'Who in your life are you most playful with?' or 'Who brings out your playful side?' Are you surprised about who first came to mind? Are you happy it is that person – or people if more than one came to mind? Who did you wish it was? Can you recall a moment or memory of shared joy between you and that person? Allow that memory to fully form in your mind. Write it down in as much detail as you can and read it aloud to yourself when you are done.

Now switch your mind to 'Who do you enjoy?' Do they feel enjoyed by you? How do you know? What opportunities for shared joy do you pursue?

Be aware of how it even feels to recall all of this. If this is a struggle for you, do you see evidence of this struggle in your life right now? Relationships with your partner, children, family, friends, colleagues – do you seek out and practise joy with them, or would you want to?

I view play as a state of mind and this joy-practice is a key part of nurturing and developing a playful state of mind. The absence of joy in our lives will wreak havoc across our physical, social, emotional and relational well-being. But because it is a practice, you can choose joy, you can flex those untoned joy muscles and build strength, flexibility and adaptability.

SO HOW DO WE CONSCIOUSLY CHOOSE AND PRACTICE JOY DAILY?

Imagine yourself feeling joyful – if you can imagine it, it can be real. Build the picture with details. Imagine yourself in your joyful scenario. Where is it? What time of day? Who is there? What are you wearing? Is there music? Who are you talking to? How do you feel there? Bring that feeling into your body. Where do you hold that joy in your body? What colour is it? What size, shape, texture? Wear something of that colour every day this week and recount that scenario.

Each day, note the thing that you are most happy or joyful about and allow yourself to reflect on one thing you wish had gone differently. Now picture how you wish it had gone and how that would make you feel. Hold that feeling in mind and body for 30–60 seconds. Take a deep breath in, imagining yourself inhaling the new positive feeling and exhale the frustrated feeling.

Give someone a compliment, perhaps about their lovely smile or a colour that really suits them, and watch how your words affect that person. Without need for reciprocation, simply share in the joy they have found in your compliment. Every morning and every evening, stand in front of a mirror in your home and pay yourself a compliment, not necessarily about how you look but about who and how you are. Compliment yourself and smile at yourself for 15 seconds.

One practical way to bring more joy into your life is to consciously and positively reframe your narrative – when you hear yourself say I have to go to work, do the laundry, take out the bins, reframe the thought to 'I get to go to work', 'I get to do the laundry'. It doesn't change what you are doing but it will gradually shift how you feel about doing it.

Remember, no blame and no shame. Give yourself permission to make mistakes and to appreciate the learning from them. Too many of us are lying awake at night unable to sleep while we run through every transgression and mistake we have ever made in our lives, and we amplify those mistakes to emotionally beat ourselves with them. Shame is stifling. Let it go… Elsa knew what she was talking about. When that blame and shame creeps up on you, hit your internal pause button and have a line you can repeat to yourself:

I made a mistake because I am human and we all make mistakes. I learned … from this mistake. I forgive myself in the way I would forgive someone else for this mistake.

Find joyful people – spend time with people who are joyful and who spark joy for you. Before the pandemic, I signed up to an evening art class – without an ounce of artistic talent I hasten to add – but it was a joyous two hours each week with people who came for lots of reasons, great conversation, laughs and a beverage and snack at the end. Find joyful people.

LET'S LAUGH

Laughter is often described as a form of 'medicine', if we understand medicine as meaning something that makes us feel better and restores us to good health. Laughter is great for our health and well-being. A good belly laugh will release residual tension we are holding in our bodies. Regular laughter boosts our overall immunity, lowers those stress hormones in our body, decreases pain and relaxes our muscles. Research has shown that living a life with lots of fun, play and laughter can increase our immune cells and infection-fighting antibodies, leaving us generally healthier. The rush of endorphins a good laugh can elicit brings an overall and generalised sense of well-being. We enjoy a good laugh but, more than that, we *thrive* on a good laugh.

Playful adults tend to find opportunities for fun in many situations, even mundane everyday tasks can be seen with a playful perspective that transforms them into something more interesting. Playful adults can often find a way to make serious situations less stressful. That said, playfulness is not the same thing as humour because playfulness is its own personality trait. While playful people will seek out humour, even in serious matters, it doesn't mean they don't take stuff seriously. On the contrary, playful people, because of their propensity to pick up on small details and to be attuned observers of others and the world around them, tend to be emotionally sensitive people as well. A playful state of mind opens up new perspectives on a range of different situations. This includes finding joy and embracing the opportunity for a good laugh wherever we can.

In chapter two I will speak about the darkness in play and how this is important, but of course the lightness and merriment of play is just as vital. Anything that affords us the opportunity for laughter should always be embraced. A good old belly laugh is one of the cheapest, quickest and easiest ways to release residual tension held in the body. A good belly laugh is a deep, authentic laugh, the kind that causes your body to shake, tears to come from your eyes and your facial muscles to be pulled and stretched upwards. You can't fake this kind of laugh but you *can* kickstart a laugh effect by starting with a fake laugh and keeping going until you are laughing at yourself trying to laugh.

PLAY BREAK

Laughter puddle

You will need a few others – at least one other, ideally two or more – to do this one. One of you lies on the ground and the next person lies placing their head on the first person's belly and the third person lies down placing their head on the second person's belly and so on, depending on how many you have doing this. The first person starts to laugh, a forced, loud laugh that causes their tummy to vibrate and move, which causes the head resting on it to move and then that person starts laughing in the same way and it passes along until you are all in a heap on the ground laughing.

Laughter – it's no joke... except when it is

There are serious health benefits to laughter, therefore there is also a seriousness in laughter. Similarly, there is a truth in jokes. Freud said that it is precisely the truth inherent in the joke that makes it funny. Making a joke can make it possible to say the difficult things. Perhaps this is why so-called 'inappropriate humour' circulates in the face of a tragedy. *Say what you feel and meme it!* Memes emerge very quickly online in response to world events. Indeed, people now use memes to express and channel all kinds of feelings, including fear.

Humour can help us cope with a situation we cannot control. Of course, there is also a cultural element to the use of humour. For example, in Ireland 'slagging' is a common means of expressing pride, success and celebrating some- one's achievements. A slagging is often insult-laden, rendering its application confusing to others, but in its purest form it is intended as a humorous expression of affection, acceptance and warmth. Even the narrative of what constitutes humour in our lives, our families and our cultures is a story in and of itself.

What do you find funny? What makes you laugh – a real belly laugh? When was the last time you enjoyed a really good laugh? Where were you and who were you with and what were you doing? How often do you get to do this – often enough?

If you read this and realise that it has been some time since you got to have a good laugh, allow your focus to move now to who and what in your life tends to spark this kind of joy. Can you make time and space for laughter? Perhaps start with something predictable that you know will give you that laughter release, such as (re)watching a good comedy show.

PLAY BREAK

Change it up to make it up

This is a great yet simple way to stimulate imagination and creative thinking. If you have ever tried reading something but ended up just staring at words on a page or screen, unable to absorb the meaning, this can help you to (re)connect and engage with it.

Wherever you are right now, look up and around you to find something with words that is in your eyeline. It might be a framed picture/poster on a wall, a magazine, a newspaper headline, a road sign or a sign on a train platform – anything at all will do. Play around with it by rearranging the words, adding on *and then…* to the end of it or turning it into a question. Now you will have created a new word by changing the spelling or simply the pronunciation of the word in question, extended a word or phrase into a longer story by adding the *and then…* and completing that sentence, or answered it as a question.

Take this example. I see and hear the words *Mind the gap* and, in my mind, I change it to something like *Find the gup and then… bring it back.* Now I get to imagine what a 'gup' might be: person/animal/object? What does it look like? Because I am on a mission to find it, I have to think of places my newly imagined gup is likely to be so that I can collect it and bring it back... but back to where and to whom? Is this a rescue mission? Am I an adventurer or a police officer or a concerned and helpful citizen; do I know the gup, or perhaps I own the gup? From an everyday phrase, I have given myself a giggle as I create this entirely imagined story in my head.

Think of the phrases you see on signs around you every day. In the canteen in your workplace perhaps the chalk board will always read *Today's special* and now you can question that.

Today's special? What is special about it [find the thing that is special about today]?

Today's special... but not as special as tomorrow will be because tomorrow... [now you imagine your perfect day as a story].

Slow down. No running allowed can become *Slow down? No! Running allowed.* (Read this one in a variety of tones and voices to change the meaning.)

Try it yourself.

CHAPTER TWO

Changing the Stories We Live By: The Playful Route

Growing up, I am sure you heard many stories of when your parents and the other adults in your life were young. Perhaps these were stories about their school days or what they did or did not have when they were children. We are raised on stories like these, and they help to shape who we are and how we live. We live storied lives in a storied world. Stories are central to who we are and how we live. I believe that stories are an inter-generational experience and, as such, the stories that we grow up with, about our families and the world we live in, heavily influence how we live our lives and can either mobilise or immobilise us in our lives. Shared narratives (such as those that run through our families) tend to synchronise our brains and therefore our experiences. I live as the stories I was raised on condition me to expect to live.

Stories are powerful. When I say that we can change the stories we live by, I mean that when we can tell our stories and reflect on their role in our lives, it enables a process of reflective functioning (the ability to recall things/events from our past but from a position of fresh thinking and new perspective) so that our stories can be integrated and will become a part of us rather than being apart from us, informing rather than impeding how we live.

Stories are a great route to playfulness because stories are a neural exercise in a similar way to how play is.

Stories, because of their imaginative power which fully engages all areas of the brain, have much greater impact than simply reporting facts in a linear fashion. When that engagement and memory are controlled and focused in a positive way, the brain's love for storytelling can be the key to healing and happiness. This healing can open a door to playfulness in our lives.

Storytelling evokes a strong neurological response within our brains too. For example, the tense moments in a story stimulate the production of cortisol, a stress hormone, which in this context serves to sharpen our focus on key elements of the story. More tender moments of a story stimulate the release of oxytocin, a happy hormone that elicits an empathic response from us. And of course, the *happily-ever-after* style of ending releases a surge in dopamine from the reward centre of our brain, our limbic area. Positive outcomes make us feel positive.

Our happiness and well-being are shaped by our life experiences and how we see and understand ourselves, internally and in relation to other people and within the world around us. This inner-working model (sense of self, self in relation to others, self within the world around us) is designed by the story of our lives to this point. But the remainder of our story is, as yet, unwritten. We can have a say in what the next chapter will be and moreover what kind of ending we are pursuing. But in order to take editorial control of our life stories, we must know them, what they are, who they came from, what meaning we have made of them and how they play out in the rhythms of our day-to-day lives.

Have you ever found yourself standing at the self-help section of a bookshop seeking the answer to something going wrong in your life? I have searched for *the secret*, I have decluttered my home in an attempt to declutter my life and, like millions of us, I embraced the hope that contentment really could be as simple as Scandinavian home comforts, fluffy socks and a cosy blanket. As interesting and helpful as these books can be, the route to rewriting the stories we live by does not exist within the pages of a book (not even this one). Instead, we need to reflect inwards with curiosity and creativity and allow ourselves to be open to change and being surprised by ourselves and our loved ones.

Changing the stories we live by to write our own chapter and ending means taking a new perspective on what has come before, what is happening now and where we want to travel next in our story. Changing the stories we live by relies on a playful state of mind!

Knowing the tone of our own family narrative can help shine a light on our view of the world around us and the stories we live by. Our sense of well-being is highly reliant on our family narrative – the stories we've been told, the stories we've understood and perceived, the stories we've used to pattern our behaviours.

In general, there are three overarching themes of our family stories:

1. **Ascending:** We came from nothing and look at all we have built and achieved as a family.
2. **Descending:** We had it all and lost it all, now look at us as we struggle to get by.
3. **Oscillating:** Our family has had challenging and rewarding times and through the highs and lows of it all we came through it as a family together.

We use stories in a myriad of important ways in our lives:

- To establish our identity in the world.
- To help us find meaning and purpose.
- To inform others.
- To connect over shared experiences.

- To say when we feel wronged.
- To organise our thoughts and feelings.

As much as 40% of what we say to other people involves the disclosure of personal information because when we get to talk about ourselves, we (most of us) tend to enjoy it.

Marshall Duke and Robyn Fivush set out to explore the anecdotal hypothesis that children who know a lot about their families, be that good or bad stories about them, tend to cope better in times of emotional stress and crisis. They developed a 20-question interview to explore participants' knowledge of family stories and how a high versus low level of knowledge was reflected in overt levels of confidence, articulacy and emotional level resilience. The findings were that children who know a lot about their families tend to do better in situations of stress or emotional crisis and displayed lower levels of anxiety, higher levels of self-esteem and fewer behavioural problems. They found that children with a strong inter-generational self are more confident, articulate and emotionally resilient. This research highlights the importance of a strong family narrative in developing an inter-generational sense of self as a child.

Take the test now as it applies to you. Read through the questions below one at a time and simply answer yes or no as you go through them.

DYK (DO YOU KNOW) TEST

1. Do you know how your parents met?
2. Do you know where your mother grew up?
3. Do you know where your father grew up?
4. Do you know where some of your grandparents grew up?
5. Do you know where some of your grandparents met?
6. Do you know where your parents were married?
7. Do you know what went on when you were being born?
8. Do you know the source of your name?
9. Do you know some things about what happened when your brothers or sisters were being born?
10. Do you know which person in your family you look most like?
11. Do you know which person in the family you act most like?
12. Do you know some of the illnesses and injuries that your parents experienced when they were younger?
13. Do you know some of the lessons that your parents learned from good or bad experiences?
14. Do you know some things that happened to your mother or father when they were in school?
15. Do you know the national background of your family (such as English, German, African, etc.)?
16. Do you know some of the jobs that your parents had when they were young?

17. Do you know some awards that your parents received when they were young?

18. Do you know the names of the schools that your mother went to?

19. Do you know the names of the schools that your father went to?

20. Do you know about a relative whose face 'froze' in a grumpy position because he or she did not smile enough?

Note that question 20 is there to remind us that not *everything* our families tell us is true. Also note that if you can answer yes to even one of these questions you have the start of an inter-generational narrative, something that you can pass on to the next generation of your family. If you are lucky enough to still have access to family members who can tell you some more of these stories, that is great. The stories of our family across generations can fascinate, bewilder and even haunt us to some extent but remember that we are always creating new chapters in our family narrative and these are the chapters *we* can author ourselves.

WHAT'S IN A NAME – YOUR NAME?

The story of our name is a significant part of the story we live by. Do you know the story of your own name? I mean why you are called what you are called or what you were almost called instead. Have you ever shared it with someone in your life? Note how it feels to tell this story. If you do not know the story of your name, do you still have access to your parents or a family member who may know it? Can you ask them about it? Be aware of how it feels to sit in the not knowing and reflect on your name now. What story can you tell yourself about your name and what it means and has meant to you? Let that be your name story!

Just for fun, take a few minutes now and imagine yourself being called the name your parents *almost* called you. Imagine how you would look, talk, walk, sound, dress in this alternate identity. Give yourself a job that you feel suits this other-named you and build a picture of the life for the new identity. This isn't about accuracy, this is about playful imagination. What desires are we holding to project onto our almost but not quite identities and how much of that is simply how we wish we were living now?

If you have children, consider the story of their name. I wonder if you chose the name before you met them and if that stayed their name or if you changed it when you met them or first held them in your arms. Does your child know the story of their name? Tell them and tell them often.

Let me share my own with you as an example of what I mean here. My name is Joanna. Initially my mother was drawn to the name Heidi (I definitely imagine what my Heidi self would be up to in life) but my dad really didn't like that name for me.

He wanted to name me Joan and my mother's second choice was Anna, so I am Joanna. There is compromise within my name and a great story too. I named my own child after my much-loved grandmother for her first name, and my mother for her middle name (both get called when there is trouble). My grandmother passed before my daughter was born. For me, we chose to name her in her honour as we wanted my grandmother's strength and compassion and capacity to love with a full heart to be a part of our daughter's life and I wanted a reason to say her name every day again. That said, we had two stand-by names in case she didn't suit this name when she was born. Her middle name mattered just as much to us, and my mother is as strong as she is kind, so again those traits for us are directly associated with that name. My daughter knows the story of her name and the people she is named after. I love telling it and she loves hearing it.

What about pet names? Did you have one and how did you feel about it? Pet names are most often used as a term of endearment so take a moment to reflect on who gave you yours and what that person means/meant to you.

The stories that arise from the above questions (in the Do You Know test) are intended to be shared onwards, with you also telling the same stories of and about yourself. This is how they become inter-generational.

If you have siblings or other family members that you can sit with and share what you (think you) know about your family narrative together, it can create a whole new layer to the story. When we exchange and discuss stories with others, we have the opportunity to co-construct new meanings in response to their recall and reflections as well as our own. This exchange of story allows us to fact check, identify any distortions we are holding in our interpretations that may be based on how we recall something or indeed on what we have been told about the situation. This isn't about dismissing what we recall or how we recall it but rather seeking to enhance or pad out the stories we live by.

Stories are powerful and playful. In fact, stories are, in and of themselves, a form of play. Listening to and telling stories about our lives and experiences helps us to develop relationships and fuels connection between us and the storyteller or listener because we can feel valued in how someone shares with us and listens to us. There is a comfort and joy in listening to someone we love telling us a story, no matter how old we are. We share thoughts, feelings, ideas and beliefs when we engage in storytelling, which also supports us in developing greater capacities for empathy and considering the perspectives of others. Exploring our life stories can lead to self-discovery and provide a pathway to greater insights and healing. As Jerome Bruner, an American psychologist who had special interest in cognitive and educational psychology, once said, 'Storytelling is a contextual bridge between play and written narrative.'

While storytelling is a form of play, there is another shared element between the two – that of symbolic representation. Children use imaginative and small-world play to explore their world and the experiences they have in relation to others by playing out scenarios with toy characters. Stories are another way that we use symbolic representation – that is, the ability to hold a picture of something or someone or an event that happened even when those things/people/events are not physically present or have long passed. Both play and stories share an imaginative quality in this respect and it is why I am drawing on narrative activities as playful exercises in this book.

Learning to playfully engage with stories is a valuable life skill because when a person can identify their role in their own story as well as the individual elements of their story, they can then begin to understand their lives and the world they're part of.

PLAY BREAK

Using story techniques to stimulate your imagination

Imaginative play such as this type of story play is a direct route to creativity. In fact, stories allow us to suspend the conflict between reality and creativity. In terms of nurturing a playful state of mind, being able to 'wonder' is an indispensable life skill. So take your time going through this play section and try each of these out over time.

Nurturing our imaginations through story play is a great way to prepare to challenge and change the stories we are living by. Try some of these story techniques.

Get yourself a set of storytelling dice (a set of dice that have symbols on each side) and make up some stories based on whatever comes to your mind when you roll them and see the symbols that land face up. I like to start with *Once upon a time...* because this gives permission for anything to happen – it doesn't have to be realistic and you can really let your imagination run with it. Try it out now using the below set of symbols. These are a set of Rory's Story Cubes.

A story in two halves

You will need a story buddy for this one.

Sit facing each other in close physical proximity and sustain eye contact throughout. It is not a staring competition so the eye contact should feel as comfortable and natural as when you typically look at someone while you speak.

You are each going to take turns to add a single word to build a story between you. You will have to anticipate the other person yet respond to whatever word they add on in the moment. Here is an example of such a story that I created with someone:

Once-there-was-rain-but-we-had-no-shoes-so-that-meant-wet-toes-this-resulted-in-chillblains-and-a-broken-spirit-but-we-made-a-resolution-to-learn-a-raindance-to-ensure-sunny-days-in-our-garden.

Be aware of what your instinctive next word would have been each time you add a word and how the other person's choice might be different from yours but you are able to use imagination and connection to creatively weave a new story between you.

You can also do this one on the go as it doesn't require any props. Try it sitting side by side on the train/bus or sitting in a waiting room or walking down the road together. Don't worry about others overhearing you – just think of how you are inspiring them to embrace playfulness too!

Some people are just natural, innate storytellers. A story flows easily from them, and even though you might know that they are ad-libbing or embellishing some details to enhance the story, you can go with it because it is engaging and fun to bear witness to. Some might find it hard to just ad-lib a story, but the capacity to create a story is within us, and with a little bit of structure, we can all grow that skill in ourselves.

Hijack a story

This technique involves taking a story (from a book, movie, magazine article, TV show or something you've heard) and changing some of the details to make it your own. For example:

Time frame: set the story in the Stone Age or in the future.

Location: Create a new geographical setting for the story.

Characters: Create a new character entirely or simply take one from the story and change three significant details about them.

Add a twist: Take a minor character and give them a sub-plot of their own that you make up.

Depending on how creative you want to get within this, you could write out the new story or try telling it to a friend and see if they recognise the original it is based on.

Re-storying the story

Think of a story you loved in your childhood and what it was that you loved about it. In rereading it, reconsider those themes and how they now resonate with you and what new understanding you have when you read it.

Now, write a short news-bulletin-style report on the story you have chosen as though it were a news item on the evening news:

I am reporting from the deep, dark forest where earlier today two young children were abandoned by their caregivers. These siblings, both minors so they cannot be named, stumbled around the forest until they came upon a private residence of an elderly woman. Locals say the elderly woman has lived off the grid in the forest for many years now having built her dream home, made entirely of sweets. It is alleged that the two children, perhaps hungry and scared, broke into the woman's home and caused significant damage to the property until she returned and disturbed them in the act of vandalism. It is further alleged that she detained the children in a make-shift holding until the authorities arrived. More on this story as we have it.

SURVIVING OUR CHILDHOODS AND LEANING IN TO POST-TRAUMATIC GROWTH

We have all survived being parented. This journey of survival will look and sound different for each of us. Perhaps you didn't have a very playful childhood or you grew up with parents who didn't play with you or bid to connect with you in playful and appealing ways. Perhaps it wasn't safe to play when you grew up. And it must feel safe to play because play is about safety and regulation but also about mobilised, active, risk-taking experiences that both thrill and scare us. Play may have felt too scary to take a chance on when living by the rules, or if staying quiet and invisible is what kept you safe.

I have written about trauma in chapter one when we looked at the science of play, but it is also relevant here when we explore changing the stories we live by and playfully working through some of our darker experiences, thoughts and feelings. Our experiences in our early years may have left us with post-traumatic depreciation. As we reflect on our childhood and how we experienced being parented as children and wonder how those stories echo through our present-day adult lives and relationships, it is about asking how we can move *from* post-traumatic depreciation *to* post-traumatic growth. Play helps to spark this post-traumatic growth in our lives and heal the hurts of those years so that we can move forward as playfully engaged and connected people.

How we experienced being parented is also the greatest influence on how we parent. We cannot change or undo how we were parented, but we can change how this manifests in our lives today and tomorrow, and all the tomorrows yet to come.

The transition from being the child of a parent to being a parent of a child is a massive one. This transition is an inter-generational experience. Parent*ing* will reactivate your experience of being parent*ed*.

PLAY AUDIT

Before you delve into this play audit, I want to emphasise that having gaps in your play patterns does not necessarily mean you had an unhappy or unpleasant childhood. There isn't a person among us who doesn't look back on their childhoods and wonder how it would have been had something(s) been different. This will be the same as you reflect on how things might have been had you had a more playful childhood or parents who played with you.

This is not a test or even a quiz – this is a reflection on our past to deepen our understanding of how it plays out in our present lives and, moreover, a means of making meaning of how we now live and how we might challenge and change that to live a more playful life! This play audit may even evoke more questions than answers for you, but know that when your play patterns are more impoverished than meaningful you can establish new patterns and move towards a more playful life.

Start by reflecting on what you did as a child that sparked joy for you and who you did this with. It might have been reading, drawing, climbing trees, running, singing, dancing or spending time with others. Pay attention to whether or not your fondest play memories are time spent with others or playing alone. Bring to mind a specific time you played a favourite activity and allow yourself to feel again how it felt then. Capture how long it has been since you felt like this. It can be hard to remember how you played as a child at all, never mind in this level of detail, especially if you haven't played much since childhood. However, it is worth sitting with this so that you can recall the activity and the feeling it gave you. It helps to track your play patterns and to begin to discover your own play personality and tendencies, as this will support you in selecting activities from this book that resonate with your playful persona. I will discuss these more later on but for now, we start with the reflection part.

For some of us, this further reflection will be a personal contemplative process; for others, we may benefit from meeting with a suitably qualified professional who can support us in working through these blocks. It is important that your reflective process leads to practical actions you can take to address any blocks you might be experiencing. The play techniques detailed throughout this book are intended to stimulate imagination, reflection, critical thinking, relational connection, flexible thinking, associations and meaning-making and will help you with this part of your process.

Now as you move forward with this play audit, seek to park any self-judgement as to how playful you are. This is about looking towards a more playful future life.

Part A

- What was growing up like for you?
- In what ways was your relationship with your mother similar to/different from your relationship with your father?
- How were you disciplined as a child and how did your parents make up with you afterwards? How did this make you feel at the time? How do you feel about it now?
- How were your successes celebrated in your family when you were a child?
- How were your disappointments managed in your family when you were a child?
- What is your happiest memory from your own childhood?

Part B

- Who played with you as a child?
- Do you have memories of your parents playing with and/or singing to you?

  - Can you recall a specific time this happened?
  - What was the game/song?
  - How did it feel when they played with/sang to you?

º   Or if they didn't, how does that feel to you now,
    and how might it have felt to you when you were
    young?

Did you feel free to do/be anyone or anything you wanted as a
child? How did this feel? Do you feel free to be who and what
you choose to be now? If not, why not? If yes, are you living
that life for yourself? What is in the way of you living this life now?

Bring to mind the times in your life so far that you feel you
have been the best version of yourself. What were you doing
and who were you with? (These tend to be examples of true
playful connection with self and others.)

What got in the way of you playing as a child? What gets
in the way of you playing now?

When did you stop 'playing' in your life? Why did this
happen at that time?

If you consider yourself actively playful, consider if you have
changed how you play and when this change occurred in
your life.

Have you discovered new ways to be playful in your life?
Would you like to?

Do you consider your relationships to be a source of and
space for playfulness in your life? Is this as you wish it to be?
(This is about separating our relationships that feel dutiful, i.e.
ones that take from us from ones that feel playful and give
back to us.)

Part C

- Do you feel deserving of good things in your life now?
- Do you experience fulfilment of your hopes and desires in your life now?
- When you think of someone who enjoyed you as a child, who immediately comes to mind? Is that person still in your life? Do you have others in your life who truly enjoy you and whom you enjoy in return? How do you spend time with these people/what do you do together?
- If you could go back and whisper one thing into your ear as a child, what would you say? What difference do you think this would have made to you as a child?
- If you had one wish for your life as it is right now, what would that wish be? Close your eyes, take a deep breath in through your nose and as you exhale it through your mouth, make that wish.

Now write a list of five things that bring you pleasure. These should be things that are about *you*, not about your child or any other relationship in your life and how they might bring you pleasure. Your list might include things like:

- Swimming
- Running
- Football
- Golf
- Painting/art and crafts
- Dinner with friends
- A hot stone massage/blow-dry/facial/nail treatment/haircut/hot-towel shave, etc.
- A night away alone with your partner/weekend away with friends.

Now ask yourself when was the last time you got to do each of the things that bring you pleasure. Can you build time into your week to ensure that you do at least one of these things each week? If you can't, ask yourself what needs to change/shift in order for you to be able to.

Play is a relational activity, one that is about connection not only to ourselves but to others in our lives as well. For this reason, I invite you to reflect on the relationships you have with others in your life and how a more playful approach to these relationships would strengthen and enhance the connection you have with others.

Start by bringing to your mind a key and important relationship you have in your life. The list below reflects both parenting and non-parenting relationships. Once you have it in mind, consider how you currently feel within this relationship and wonder how the other person might also feel within this relationship. Hold in mind that you are making an inference as to how they might feel, meaning you might be right and you might be wrong. You can only express certainty over your own feelings. Also note that if you are applying this to how you parent and you have more than one child, you will have to repeat this for each child – every child is different and how you parent each of them will also be at least slightly different.

Ask yourself the following questions:

- Do I regularly show appreciation for this person? How do they know that I appreciate them?
- *Re children:* Do I find opportunities each day to tell my child that I love them and that I am proud of them?
- Do we have shared as well as separate interests? How do I feel about this?
- *Re children:* Do I find opportunities to encourage them to practise independence? Am I developing these opportunities in line with their development?
- Is this relationship one with healthy boundaries? What do those look/feel like? How would I like this to look and feel like?
- *Re children:* Am I able to be firm yet gentle with my child when necessary?

- Am I safe, reliable, calm and consistent in how I turn up in this relationship?

- *Re children:* Am I safe, predictable, calm and consistent in how I interact with and respond to my child?

- Do we each get what we need from this relationship in terms of support, connection, celebration. Do I shine a light on what the other person needs from me and do they do this for me?

- *Re children:* Do I follow my child's lead where possible but take charge when necessary?

- Do I have the opportunity to laugh at least once a day with this person? Do they feel that I enjoy them?

- Do I express interest in their day, regardless of how my own day was?

- *Re children:* Do I seek to know the best bit of my child's day and what bit of their day they would like to change?

- Am I interested in what interests this person?

- Do I encourage them to push themselves, even a little, beyond their comfort zone to reach for something they want or to try something new?

- *Re children:* Do I encourage my child to try new things and to take (appropriate) risks?

- Do I celebrate them in times of failure as well as success?

- *Re children:* Do I praise their efforts over any outcomes?

- Do I show empathy when this person seeks my help/support/protection and comes to me for comfort/solace?

- Do I feel safe and secure in this relationship to know that we can find our way back to each other when we pull apart (in tension/row)?

- *Re children:* Did I experience repair/recovery following a rupture with my child today (perhaps not every day)?

- Are we playful together? Do I bid to playfully engage with this person?

- *Re children:* Do I play with my child for 15 minutes each day?

- *Re children:* Do I ensure we have a bedtime story together each night no matter what else has/hasn't happened?

A self-audit is not a one-time reflection. This is an exercise that you can and should repeat as your relationship (to self and others) grows and evolves.

DEAR ME (THEN, NOW AND YET TO BE)...

One of the questions I have asked above is what would you like to go back and whisper into your own ear as a child and what difference this would make. I am now inviting you to take this a step further and to write to yourself. You can choose to do this by writing one of these letters or perhaps you will write all three letters. You do not have to sit and do all three in a single sitting (unless that works for you – I would find that a lot personally).

1. Write a letter to your child-self. Reflect and seek to make meaning of experiences within your relationship with your parents at a time when you could not make meaning of them.

2. Write a letter to your present-time self. Reflect on how the relationships in your life are impacting on you, your well-being, your life. Encourage yourself to embrace opportunities to be more playful so also include why you think this matters to you in your life at this time.

3. Write a letter to your future self. Describe the type of relationships you want to bring into your life, emphasise the time and space for more playfulness and set yourself an outlook on life in your future.

The past is vague enough for you to choose any age/stage of childhood that seems most pertinent for you and the same applies to the future – you can decide how far into the future you want to visualise. The present should be reflective of the right here, right now.

BUSTING THOSE PLAY MYTHS – PLAY IS FOR EVERYONE

Play looks and sounds different in each of us. Playful people have the capacity to move with the up and down swing of the emotional regulatory rollercoaster. Our emotional regulation isn't a straight line, be that a hyper- or hypo-aroused line. Our emotional arousal is much more like a wave (not a spike) that moves through highs and lows in our day. What we aim for is that this wave doesn't push too far out of our *window of tolerance.*

We all have a window of tolerance – it is where we feel comfortable and in control. For most of us, by adulthood, this window is a fairly decent size and even when we get heightened and agitated, we don't lose it!

Imagine you are running late, sitting in traffic and just as you are about to move through a junction, a car in the line beside you cuts across, meaning you miss the light. You might lean on your car horn, swear, shout out loud, you may even snap at whoever might be in the car with you at the time (because we do not make good choices or decisions in this heightened state of arousal). But most of the time, you might honk your horn and grit your teeth (or swear a little) but will stop yourself going any further by employing the regulation strategies you have developed. Perhaps you turn off talk radio, as that narrative is stressing you out, you roll down the window for some air and take a deep breath. You are self-regulating within your window of tolerance.

Equally, there will be days or part of every day when your energy drops very low and you begin to feel lethargic and even forgetful. But again, catching yourself walking into the kitchen and forgetting why you came in is a sign to employ your more upward regulating strategies to stay regulated. Perhaps you make a cup of tea and eat a biscuit, walk outside and move around the building/garden to get some energy back into your body. Whatever your strategies are, you have things that you know you can do when you feel revved up or sluggish, and most of the time these will work well for you to ensure that even when you start to feel uncomfortable, you are not out of control.

When we are children we rely on our parents/caregivers to co-regulate us from their bigger window of tolerance to help and support us in extending our immature window of tolerance. Positive, playful, connected experiences extend and grow that window of tolerance, whereas stressful, toxic and traumatic experiences shrink and compress it. A wide window of tolerance enables us to stay comfortable even when we feel challenged, it enables us to stay emotionally connected (to self and others) even when we experience highs and lows in our day, and it reflects our capacity to manage the emotional stresses life throws our way.

One of the greatest tools we have at our disposal to help safeguard against mental stress (not mental illness as that is an entirely separate entity) is to increase our capacity for playful engagement and connection with ourselves, others in our lives and within the world around us. Play is essential in helping us (regardless of age) to reach our potential and understand who we are as people. Play helps us to loosen up, challenge the way things are in our lives, especially if they are not serving us well, and create a new way of doing things that better serve us.

PLAY WITH THIS – WOULD YOU RATHER…? ACTIVITY

This is a great activity to stimulate imagination and start embracing silliness while helping us to understand and be understood by each other in a deeper and more playful way.

Take turns asking each other a series of *would you rather* questions, increasing the level of wonderfully wacky options as you progress:

- Would you rather only be able to sing every time you spoke or not be able to stop speaking forever more?
- Would you rather lose your hearing or your taste?
- Would you rather have mucus drip from your nose all day or from your ear all night?

- Would you rather only be able to smell farts or for everything you eat to taste gone off?
- Would you rather live as a horse or a dog?
- Would you rather have to cycle or swim everywhere you go?
- Would you rather have a lizard's tongue or an elephant's trunk for a nose?

Try your own and really stretch your creativity with this one. Ask each other why for every choice made.

Play fuels connection in the parent–child relationship but in truth it is something that is pertinent in *all* human relationships. Play allows us to explore and even establish who we are as individuals, who we are in relation to others, who we are together. It will also allow us to find our identity within the world around us. Play strengthens and enhances our connections. In other words, play brings us closer together. It is also essential in enabling relational repair following a rupture.

A JOURNEY FROM RUPTURE TO REPAIR

I invite you to paint a picture in your mind now by thinking back to a row you have had with someone you care about, someone you consider yourself to have a good relationship with. This can be from a recent experience or something that comes to mind from your childhood or adolescence. Think about the moments before the row sparked, think of what was happening (emotionally) for you during the row, and think about the aftermath. What were you left holding (emotionally) afterwards? What was your dominant feeling afterwards?

Now move to thinking about how you negotiated the repair following this rupture. Who said what, who instigated it, how did you speak about the repair and how did you 'do' it (think of gestures more than words)? When we playfully approach repair, it is about how we 'do' that communication rather than how we speak it. When you take this approach you will find that often it is a tentative gesture, perhaps an offer of a cup of tea, a casual remark about a news story or event, maybe there is then a hug of some kind or an overt *I'm sorry…* and then what? How quickly do you move to something light and playful to elicit a smile or even a laugh between you after a row? A shared moment of joy that tells you that you are back on track relationally, back to being connected?

PLAY AS A RELATIONAL EXPERIENCE/THE RELATIONAL EXPERIENCE OF PLAY

I was compiling a list of toys from my childhood as part of a homework assignment my child was doing comparing toys from nowadays to 'long ago' (I will pretend that I wasn't defensive at the idea that my childhood toys were from long, long ago) and as I was sitting and thinking of what I liked to play with as a child, I was struck that what came to mind wasn't just a 'toy' but a memory of how I played and who I played with. It was easier to recall *who* I played with rather than *what* I played with. For example, even when I did remember a toy, it came with a memory of who among my siblings or friends also had one of these or a different character in the collection and how we played together.

Play is a relational experience. Yes, there is definitely value in playing alone and time spent in that glorious daytime reverie of imagination and imaginative play, but given that play is a language, a means of communicating and making meaning of our experiences, there is only so much value to essentially talking to yourself. You also need people to talk with and people to play with. We are drawn to play with those we find we can relate to. It is the reassurance of seeing someone enjoy what we also enjoy. There is such comfort and connection to be found in the recognition of our own feelings about something reflected back to us through someone else we are sharing that moment with.

One of the best ways to reconnect with play is to recall what we enjoyed playing with as children and then to try to immerse ourselves in *how* that felt for us then. Recalling toys I enjoyed playing with in childhood also inspired me as an adult to see if some of that same play would re-spark a familiar joy in me. This is something we can all try out and I encourage you to do so in a few different ways.

If you are someone who has managed to salvage a box of your old toys from the attic of your family home or the back of the garage/shed, dust them off and sit and play with them. Start by playing with them in the way you recall enjoying and see if something more authentic is ignited in doing so. It can be surprisingly cathartic to have a chat with your old doll/ teddy who was your early childhood confidante or to pick up some Sylvanian family characters and have them play out a little scene while you speak their voices aloud for them.

If you don't have access to toys from your childhood, are there any items available to you now that you might have played with as a child? Let me get you started.

A hula-hoop: Stand in your kitchen, living room or garden. Wherever you can get your hula on. Take a few minutes every day to practise hula-hooping and challenge yourself to spin a little longer each day.

A skipping rope: Find a space just as above and challenge yourself to skip non-stop for as long as you can. I found that singing a skipping rhyme in my head while doing this was a good distraction from how incredibly unfit and uncoordinated I felt restarting my skipping. Once I had built up some stamina, I changed my focus to counting my skips, mixing it up with some rope twists and then using a sand timer to skip for set amounts of time – fun and fitness all at once.

Chalk: Take some chalk and draw out a hopscotch template on your patio/drive/pavement outside your home. Have some fun working your way up through the board.

Ball: Take a ball and practise your keepie-uppies, kicking it against a wall but adding in a jump/jumping jack/hop/twist while you wait for it to rebound back to you, not breaking the streak. Or play kerbs with the ball (stand on one side of the road, being road safe of course, and throw the ball so that it hits the edge of the other kerb and bounces back to your half of the road again… repeat).

These are all activities that you can do alone but also that you can do with another person or a few others to increase the fun. If you have two others you can add some challenge into that skipping activity by having your play partners turn the rope while you jump the middle. Mix it up further by taking turns and the person who jumps the middle must do so while holding a cup of water. The person with the most water still in their cup at the end is the winner. Kerbs can be played with two on opposite sides of the road, and the ball rebound game can be played with as many people as you have, each taking turns to catch/kick the rebound back to the wall and not break the streak.

So, a hula-hoop, a skipping rope, a ball and simple chalk will offer a way to re-experience play for all of us.

I think that singing is a great way to express emotions and to get us out of our busy cognitive minds, affording us some escapism and fantasy as we can imagine ourselves on a stage or tap-dancing through the rain. And you do not have to be 'good' at singing to enjoy and draw benefit from it. When we sing, we are playing with our voices, using our prosody to provide context, give meaning to words, thoughts and feelings. The prosody of our voice, that musicality of voice we have, is one of the best ways we can convey what we are thinking and feeling to others. As well, it is a key way of engaging and connecting with others. So, why *say* it when you could *sing* it?

I have always loved musicals. Far from being horrified at the prospect of living in a world where people would randomly burst into song or a perfectly coordinated dance routine, I rather think that I would love it! Something I enjoy doing when I am feeling very mind-cluttered or have had one of those days/weeks where I have been up in my head far too long is plotting out a real-life musical. Stick with me on this, even if you hate musicals, and give this one a go.

THE BROADWAY ACTIVITY

If I have had a particularly stressful week or if there has been a specific life event causing that stress, I sit and imagine the week/event as though it were a musical. I break it into three acts, which is a way of breaking something that might feel large and overwhelming into more manageable sections. Then I roughly script out a story with what characters will be in it and what the task in the story will be, who/what will get in the way, who/what will help the main character, what the drama high point is and how it will all end. Then I scroll through my Spotify and I select a variety of songs that fit with the theme and characters in my story. I add into my rough script where each song would appear and for what character. I even make it into a playlist and then listen to it in order, maybe lying on my bed or going outside for a walk while I imagine my story and the various scenes as I do so. This all helps me to break an event down into components that are more manageable, and by playfully exploring individual elements and the people involved, I gain deeper insight into what happened but also how I feel about what happened, and I might even see a solution to the challenge at hand, though that isn't my specific goal here.

An alternative way to do this is to take someone else's life, someone famous who you know quite a bit about and use Spotify to design the playlist for the musical of their life. Pick anyone you like from the past or present, a person of historical standing, a politician, a singer, actor, activist or other celebrity.

IMAGINING OUR WAY TO A STRESS-FREE LIFE

Imaginative expression can provide some much-needed light relief from the pressures of the world we live in. It is about using imaginative play to process real-life stresses. When reality looms large and overwhelming in our lives, it is our capacity to laugh, question, wonder and imagine that will save us.

Play, especially imaginative play, allows us to take control of a situation that threatens to control us. Pause here for a moment and consider if you have ever had an unpleasant exchange, experience or encounter with someone, and in the moment you didn't say much but as soon as you were away from them you had a full-blown stand-off – in your imagination. In our imaginations, we win that fight every time! It is the same as an open letter that tends to start with something like 'Dear person who stole my parking space' or 'Dear stranger who passed a remark about my child's behaviour in the supermarket' or 'Dear school bully, here is what you didn't realise…' These letters say everything the writer couldn't say to the actual person, offering a catharsis within a controlled mechanism – controlled because the other person doesn't talk back in the imaginative fight/monologue/ one-sided letter. This allows us to take imaginative control of the situation. We reverse the scenario, assume the dominant role and re-script what happened in the safety of our own contained space later on.

OPEN LETTER ACTIVITY

Try writing an open letter of your own. Pick someone who crossed you but who you didn't feel that you could stand up to or assert yourself to in the moment. It could be a stranger or someone you know. Write out your 'Dear person who' letter (you don't necessarily need to share it publicly). As you write it, bring to mind the person you are writing to, imagine what it would feel like to say all of this to them and capture how that feels inside you. As an extra step, consider writing a *P.S.* to your letter, a short paragraph starting, 'Dear person who, this is what it has felt like to write you this letter even though you will never read it…' to bring your reflection right up to the present moment.

NO ONE TO PLAY WITH

In this book, I am sharing lots of play prompts, invitations to play alone and also with others. We need both sets of skills in our lives. But play is a practice and needs to be a daily practice in each of our lives. If we have survived a childhood where opportunities to play were scarce and restricted (remembering that it has to feel safe to play) then we have likely reached adulthood prioritising seriousness above all else, a life of creative frustrations. When we have grown up with no one to play with, we have not learned to play. Yet. I want to be clear that I mean *not yet*. Play is always possible, the potential to access a playful state of mind is there for all of us, but we have to know how to get there and to believe that we deserve it when we do.

Case study

Laurie is a 35-year-old woman who reached out to me after she saw me give a TV interview where I brought the interviewers into a cotton-ball snowball fight at the end. Her initial email to me said she was frozen looking at me do this. She found it enticing and terrifying all at once and said she rewound that part of the interview a number of times trying to work out what made it possible for three grown adults to behave like children on national TV. She was genuinely perplexed and at times in our first session, she was even angry with me for 'making out like that behaviour is normal for adults when it isn't'. Over the course of our work together, Laurie described a very serious childhood. Her parents were devoted to Laurie and her siblings doing really well in life. She explained that this meant an expectation that they excelled at school, studied at home and took on a huge amount of extra-curricular activities, all aimed at making them highly skilled. There was no TV at home, and evenings were spent studying, reading or practising music. There was little to no time to play as they were always occupied and busy. Besides, she added, her parents thought play was a waste of their time when they could have been 'bettering' themselves.

Laurie struggled to feel frustrated or angry with her parents. Every criticism she passed was immediately corrected by evidencing how well she and her siblings had done in their lives. When I invited her to tell me what doing well looked like now as adults she described high-level, well-paid careers, owning homes in attractive suburbs and that she could 'still play concert-level piano if ever called on to do so'. She wasn't often called on to do so.

There was no evidence of fun, joy or relational connections in her life. She described meeting up with her parents as a status update whereby she would advise them of what she had achieved since they last met and they would appraise her outcomes with suggestions as to how she could do better.

Laurie had almost no experience of play in her childhood, that is, of playing and being played with. She was very sensitive to any inference that her parents had not done right by her. This was an inference that came from Laurie from time to time and not one that I made. Laurie only dealt in absolutes, evidence-based and fact-checked exchanges. It was not possible for her to see that her parents loved her very much and still fell short in terms of how they parented her, denying her the right to play and to access imaginative expression as she grew up. In her mind, they either loved her and were therefore the best kind of parents or *they were bad parents who couldn't have loved her.*

Quite quickly, I could see that for me to reach Laurie, we would have to come at this in a way that wasn't about speaking or pure talk therapy. Talk therapy relies on the part of the brain associated with executive function, reasoning and rational thought being accessible, but when living with trauma or distressing life events, that part of the brain can become inaccessible, rendering us 'stuck' in the process. I needed to take a more bottom-up (brain-stem upwards) rather than top-down (neocortex-downwards) approach using sensory input (doing/playing) to co-regulate and soothe the parts of her brain that were preventing her from making deeper and more reflective connections within her own story.

We started with 15-minute sequences of playful activities that I led her through. After 15 minutes we would pause and breathe and process aloud what that experience had been like for her. Sometimes she could speak to that experience, sometimes she cried and said nothing, and sometimes she

*became very angry and would accuse me of wasting her
time. When I sought to make meaning of these feelings she
would often cancel or simply not show up to the next one
or two sessions. When I named this pattern to her, she froze
and asked, 'Are you saying I am having a tantrum? I AM
NOT HAVING A TANTRUM.'*

*I sat with this outburst, reflected that I wasn't saying
that but was curious to understand if she had ever thrown
tantrums as a child (very developmentally healthy and
normal) and what would happen when she did this. Laurie
recounted painful stories of how what was deemed bad
behaviour was responded to by her parents. She felt her
emotional outbursts were deeply shaming, because she had
been deeply shamed in response to her typical childhood
behaviour growing up. At this point, Laurie, who had
presented as a very controlled person, began to present as
an angry, pouty and at times sulking child or teenager in
our sessions. Any and all attempts to playfully connect were
met with her ridicule and derision, sometimes an exasper-
ated and exaggerated eye-roll and some passive resistance
whereby she would sabotage the activity rather than engage
with me in it.*

If we come from a *wounded family system* it can be very difficult to trust safe connections even when they do present
themselves to us. This is a family where play was ridiculed,

tantrums laughed at and dismissed and now as adults even stories from that time are not believed, attempts to challenge and change and to do something in a new or different way are rejected and met with hostile derision: *who do you think you are?/that's far from how we were raised/I am so embarrassed for you.* The absence of playful connection within the family system has resulted in a tone of rejection, suspicion and aggression. It is frustrating and can be enraging too, and this kind of rage stifles us, consumes us and blocks the flow of emotional expression and therefore creative expression. When it is like this, unprocessed, pervasive and engulfing anger short-circuits our capacity to play and be creative. We feel numb and our energy drops to a purely functional level, just enduring life, not enjoying it.

You need to have had moments when someone significant in your life was there to nurture, encourage and enjoy your play with you, certainly in childhood but ideally also throughout adolescence and into adulthood. Someone who celebrated your efforts, delighted in your creativity and made you feel entitled to play. As illustrated in the case study, the child who has no one to play with can grow into a hostile adult unless there is an intervention that can challenge and change this.

Laurie and I continued to work together and I welcomed her anger, her derision, her distress and her fear as it presented itself within our 15-minute play sequences. A lot of the types of play I am referring to are included in this book for you all to try too.

At one point, Laurie reflected that no one had ever sung to her, not as a child, not ever. I asked her if it would be okay if I sang to her. She giggled nervously but said, 'Go on then, sing to me.' I held her gaze in mine as I sang, 'Twinkle, twinkle, little star, what a special girl you are, hair so dark, soft pink cheeks and big bright eyes from which you peek. Twinkle, twinkle little star, what a special girl you are.'

There was about 35 seconds of total silence when I finished and she stared at me, slowly blinking silent tears down her cheeks. We held the silence so that she could feel exactly how she felt in that moment. She sighed loudly, smiled softly and whispered, 'So that's what that's like then.'

This wounded system can play out in other systems and other environments too. The workplace can embody this as its culture and become a toxic place where bullying and harassment are rampant. It can (and does) play out in political systems too. When one side dismisses the lived experiences of another side, rejects their stories as exaggerated and not real (i.e. not to be believed or acted on) we get a polarised us/them or included/excluded split within a society. When we cannot hear each other's stories as our individual and collective truth and accept them as such, when we can only feel safe and strong when others are struggling and weak, we are not connected as a society. Without that connection, we cannot play together and will instead attack and deride each other.

FALLING IN AND OUT OF SYNCH – THE PROCESS OF RE-ESTABLISHING CONNECTION

Of course, all of these systems, be they family, work or societal, will never be perfectly 'in synch'. Playful connection doesn't rely on us all being in synch all of the time – far from it. Synchrony is a process in itself, and it is precisely the being in synch (connected) then falling out and being out of synch (disconnected/disrupted) and then getting back into synch (re-establishing connection) that contributes to a robust and resilient system. Within that process of 'getting back into synch' there is immense learning. We have the opportunity to hear and be heard, to consider a situation from more than our own point of view and look at alternative solutions. This is precisely how we strengthen connectivity between people within any system.

Laurie and I gradually moved from our play-based sessions to a blend of play and talking, and from there to more talk-based sessions with some playfulness included. We found that over the duration of treatment, Laurie began to seek out playful spaces and connections in her life, and as she did that, she needed and sought them less in the room with me. We had been working with playful ways to work through her anger, aggression and often unrealistically high standards she held others (including colleagues) to. She took up tag-rugby and was a natural in that arena. It was a form of play that blended collaboration and competitiveness and offered a healthy and playful way to release the simmering tension and aggression she held in her body.

Having spoken about how she hated her piano as she had never really grown to love it when she was playing 'centuries-old music for some examiner to grade her on', I was intrigued when she told me she had joined a community ukulele group which gathered weekly to play all kinds of songs. Music (rhythm and synchrony) triggers the sub-systems of our brain associated with emotional regulation and, indeed, playing within a musical group brought Laurie a great deal of pro-social benefits.

As she integrated more playfulness into her life, she softened and opened up more in our work about the life she wanted to live and the story she wanted her life to tell. She moved to a new job and area and as such our work began to wind down.

On our second-last session she told me, 'I did it! The thing that brought me to you at the very start. Well, I did it!'

She meant the cotton-ball snowball fight. She laughed as she spoke of being at a party in someone's house and at a certain part of the night when games began (Cards Against Humanity, Twister, drinking games) she had suggested a snowball fight and it had been a roaring success with everyone howling with laughter around her.

'I can have fun, I can be silly, I can be fun.'

I am not suggesting that play is, in and of itself, enough to address unresolved childhood trauma. I am a trauma specialist and use a blended modality approach to working with people who have experienced trauma. In order for us to access Laurie's capacity to interweave some of those very early implicit memories with a narrative that would enable her to make new meaning of them and move forward with fresh thinking and a new perspective on her life, we had to start with that sensory input, the play that would enable us to co-regulate the parts of her brain preventing her from being able to otherwise speak things she didn't yet have the words to say. The play was transformative.

One of the things I have mentioned in Laurie's case is that she presented as defended, aggressive, angry, even enraged at times. I wanted to speak directly to these feelings in a way that would be playful and safe for her to begin to express this part of herself. Challenge play is a great way to do this. Challenge isn't about conflict; it is about engagement that is collaborative (working together to achieve a task) more than competitive (though some degree of competition can be fun and playful too) and this kind of playfulness can stimulate connection and strengthen solution-focused thinking as well.

CHALLENGE PLAY FOR GROWN-UPS

Tug-of-war: You need a play partner for this one. Hold a rope or long piece of material (e.g. a scarf) between you and pull away from each other. Increase the challenge by each taking one hand off and pulling only with one hand. Now, raise your thumb on the hand still pulling. This is steadily increasing the challenge within the activity. You can repeat this using your non-dominant hand on the second round and raising the thumb on that one too. Be aware of how it feels within you when the task gets increasingly challenging. Does it scare you or excite you? What thoughts come with this feeling? Are you likely to grit your teeth, clench your jaw and dig in harder with your feet while you take the strain into your shoulders or do you feel the urge to let go, respond to the strain in your body by saying enough, I'd rather lose the game than hold this tension? Neither is better or worse – it is about using the activity to better understand how you respond to challenge from an embodied perspective. What is instinctually aroused within you when confronted with challenge?

Take aim and fire: Sit on the floor and place a cup or bowl about 1 metre away to start and then increase the challenge each time by increasing the distance between you and the cup. Beside you have a cotton ball, ping-pong ball, a coin, a spoon and other things of different weight but all should be small sized so think of things like a fun-sized chocolate bar. Sit on the floor, take aim and see how many you can get straight into the cup or as close to the cup as you can.

Next time you are making yourself a cup of tea, squeeze and put the teabag to one side. When the cup is empty, sit again and take aim to fire that teabag into the cup from 1 metre, then 2 metres and keep going until you start missing.

Now, if you *really* want to step up the challenge level of this one, take a slice of bread, stand about 1 metre away (you can start closer and build up distance, as above) and toss that bread aiming to get it straight into the slot of the toaster. This level is significantly more challenging but some of us really enjoy challenge play, so this one is for you.

Be aware what your initial thoughts are as you read through this challenge. If it is *a spoon? into a cup? that will chip* or *not a teabag, that would stain!* it shows that challenge play brings up a level of caution in you. That is perfectly okay. Omit the spoon and teabag and play it another way. It doesn't mean this activity isn't for you – it means that you will find more comfortable ways to play it. If you immediately think of ways to increase the level of challenge by standing on a chair and throwing from both distance and height at the same time or digging out your balance board and trying to stabilise your balance while throwing, you can reflect on how challenge play excites you and encourages you to push the boundaries and increase the level of risk.

RISK – WILL YOU TAKE A RISK ON RISK-TAKING?

I know that much of what I suggest in here in terms of how I advocate for play in our adult lives can feel risky for many of us. If this is you then I really appreciate you reading this book because it says that you are (even a little) open and curious about embracing a more playful approach to your mental well-being. Play, especially when we have not really played in a long time, can indeed feel unsafe and risky because I am inviting you to take a chance on something entirely new. I understand that. Risk, while often uncomfortable, is in fact an essential part of our lives, and play can be one of the safest ways to explore how we relate to risk in how we live.

The groundwork for our relationship to risk begins in early childhood and we must grow it in line with our development throughout our lives. Risk-taking behaviour is making a choice or taking an action when the outcome of that choice or action is unknown and cannot be fully predicted. It involves anything with an inherent chance of success or failure from the outset, which you decide to do anyway. From our early childhood onwards, risk-taking can evolve into making new friends, joining a sports team, learning a new skill. Risk-taking can also play out more negatively in behaviours such as problematic eating/drinking, lying and cheating.

In life, at all ages including adulthood, we need access to healthy risk-taking behaviour to provide us with the adrenalin and psycho-social benefits risk-taking affords. These benefits include boosting confidence, supporting development of new skills and new learning, stimulating creativity and solution-focused thinking, gaining mastery over challenges and affording us opportunities for pride in our accomplishments in a way that encourages us to take on new experiences and challenges without fear of failure. If we don't engage in healthy risk-taking behaviour, the pull of negative risk-taking behaviour will be all the stronger, with no alternative action.

THE THREE STAGES OF DEVELOPMENTAL PLAY

Risk-taking behaviour is the convergence of two motivational systems. One system renders a person sensitive to punishment while the other renders a person sensitive to reward. Play is ultimately what enables us to regulate and balance the two systems. There are three key stages of developmental play that we each need to have had access to during our early childhood and indeed beyond. As you read these, cast your mind back to your own childhood and see if you can bring to mind experiences of each of these stages of play. If you can't and you still have access to your parents or other family members who would recall you well from this period of your life, ask them if they might recall you playing like this as a child. I am including reference to the type of life/social skills each stage affords us and you can identify if you might have any gaps in these skills. I am also including a reference to the approximate age for each stage but please read this as a developmental age rather than a chronological one. I will then make suggestions as to how you can repeat these stages in your life now as an adult.

Let us look now at those stages of play.

Stage one: infancy to 3.5 years old

What is it? This is that stage of messy, tactile sensory play including sand, water, bubbles, Play-doh and music. This is play that sees a child more fascinated with the box the toy came in than the toy itself because boxes are all about containment and discovering what is on the inside rather than the outside. This is the stage of play where we start to understand that we have a skin that not only contains and holds us together but shows us where we end and the world and people outside us begin. This is where we start to appreciate a sense of self and awareness of others.

Why does it matter? Messy play is really important because when our caregiver can tolerate, enjoy and invite our external mess and chaos in a way that shows us that they can organise, manage and contain it, we learn that we can also bring our internal mess and chaos to this person who will help us to make meaning of it. Even when they don't understand it, they will stay with us in the mess until we can both understand what may not make sense to either of us initially. It teaches us that we can be contained and held and can position ourselves safely in a world and with people beyond ourselves and our little home bubble.

How do I re-experience this type of play now in adulthood? Sensory play in adulthood can help us to maintain a strong connection with our sense of self and to read when we are internally in or out of synch. It can elicit positive feelings, promote relaxation and generally impact our mood and well-being in a positive way.

- Sensory box: Take a small keepsake-size box or something no bigger than a shoebox. Put a variety of sensory items in the box, from things like perfume/after-shave samples, small scented candles/wax melts, a container of sand (I use an old camera-roll container for mine), a piece of material (I have both silk and velvet in mind), nice hand cream that you can apply, something chewy, sucky and crunchy (Haribo, pretzel, lemon sherbet sweet). I also have a small kaleidoscope that I picked up in a trinket shop but you could have a small view-finder toy (basically something for your sense of sight), some small smooth pebbles and shells, and something squeezy or stretchy (such as a fidget toy). I also have a small wind-up music toy that plays a lullaby-type song. You can make your own but ensure that there is something for each of your senses in here.

- Cooking: This can be a very sensory experience. Cooking engages sight, smell, touch and taste and the noises of baking equipment or sizzling food engage our auditory sense as well.

- Food art: Save your veggie peelings and before you turn them into veggie stock for your freezer, play with them. Create art out of the veggie peelings, transforming carrot peelings into hair, onion skins into ears, a broccoli stem into a nose and so on, or create a more scenic picture out of your food art on a board. You could also take a few minutes at the start of your dinner to rearrange the food on your plate into a scene or an expression.

- Sensory bath: The hot water, bubbles, scented bath oil, dimmed lights, candle and soft music all combine to provide a rich and relaxing sensory experience.

- Hand massage: Take some hand cream and apply it to one hand at a time. Starting by taking your left hand in your right hand, turn and notice any marks on your hand. Perhaps there is a paper cut, a birthmark, a bruise or a freckle. Look at your fingers – are they soft or dry? As you turn your hand over, look at and trace the lines on your palm with the index finger of the other hand. Notice where the lines converge, which is deepest or longest. Apply the cream and massage it in slowly, using the kind of deep but pleasurable pressure that works for you. Pull up along each finger, one at a time and massage into the cuticles of your nails. Repeat on the other hand.

- Cuddle up cosy and warm: Put on your cosiest lounge-wear (loose tracksuit bottoms and a hoodie, etc.) and wrap a soft warm blanket or your duvet around you while you curl up on the sofa. Feel your body supported by cushions and snuggle in deeply. Watch a comfort movie (whatever that means to you) and eat a snack like popcorn as you do. Turn off your phone and ensure that you give and take this time for yourself.

- Sip and ground: Make a hot beverage of your choosing in your favourite mug (we all have one) and take it outside. Feel your feet flat on the ground, lift your toes up and rest them down and rock from heel to toe and back again. Hold your mug with both hands and allow yourself to feel the heat seep into your skin. Bring the mug up to your face and inhale the smell deeply. Take a sip and hold it in your mouth for just a few seconds before you swallow, really savouring the temperature and taste as you do.

Stage two: 3.5–5.5 years old

What is it? This is where we start to deepen our understanding of the world outside ourselves by beginning to take in and consider the perspectives of others. This is the stage where we play with little dolls/dinosaurs/cars (small-world-type play) and have them talk to and interact with each other. In this stage of play we are able to do two or more voices as we play out the characters engaging with each other and responding to each other.

Why does this matter? This means we are playing with holding two or more perspectives in mind at the same time. Being able to consider the perspectives of others is essential to developing empathy, critical thinking, reciprocity and general civility. It is the beginning of us being able to project outside ourselves and mentalise what others might be thinking or feeling, and later we will strengthen this to being able to change behaviour to elicit a different or preferred response. We can begin to make meaning of scenarios and situations and see that there is more than one way, our way, of experiencing something.

How do I re-experience this type of play now in adulthood?
A lot of the play I included when we were considering our storied lives would also apply here but also consider these activities:

- One-minute speech making: While you can do this one alone and set a timer on your phone or use a one-minute sand timer, it is more fun to play with others, and this is a more-the-merrier-type of activity. Write out a variety of random topics from country names, political topics, popular culture, current news stories, climate matters, household items/inanimate objects, food. Fold each slip of paper up and take turns picking one from the bowl holding them. Now speak about this topic for one minute non-stop. You get bonus points if you don't pause, repeat yourself or say 'uh' or 'erm' while doing it.
- A local plot: Using the name of your street/housing estate where you grew up, the first other place that you moved to when leaving home and where you currently live,

make a list of all of the words. Now arrange them into a book or movie title with a short synopsis. For example, when I do this I am left with these words, *Shamrock, Sea, Vale, Shrewsbury, Valley, Temple, Road* and I can produce, *The Tale of Shamrock the Shrew, Buried at Sea.*

- Create a character: Think of a really good book you recently read or a movie/TV show you recently saw. It should be something you loved and thought about afterwards or couldn't wait to discuss with someone else who had seen or read it. Once you have it in mind, create a new character to slot into the plot. Give them a name, character traits, a part in the plot, a relationship to someone else in the plot. Consider what they look like (maybe draw them) and how their addition would change the outcome of the plot – is it better or worse?

- I've got something to tell you: Write out a dialogue (this is great if you can act it out with someone else) between two people that starts with the line, '*I've got something to tell you…*' Take that as line one for one of the people in your conversation and they can each only have a maximum of ten lines each.

Stage three: 5.5–7 years old

What is it? This is role play but as dramatic play rather than dressing-up play. This type of play is where the play decides what the prop is (e.g. a scarf is never just a scarf: it is a magic carpet, a picnic blanket, a bandage, a blanket for a baby or a cape for a superhero) rather than the prop deciding what the play is, such as wearing a princess dress that makes me that princess and nothing else. In stage-three play, we learn how to push boundaries (or perhaps refine the skills already developing) and test out what it would be like if we were in other roles in our lives, be that playing at being a parent or a doctor, a teacher, a musician or a builder. This is a dramatic stage of play and, as such, should never be taken literally. As children, our being the meanest teacher or parent we could conjure up wasn't a literal reflection of the parent or teacher we grew up with. We are stretching ourselves and testing limits to see how big and bad we could be if we were in charge, how much could we get away with and what would it be like if *we* ruled the world.

Why does it matter? Everything we take in during stage-one play, we push out in stage-two play onto the little objects in small-world play and now we insert ourselves into this in stage-three play. There is always evidence of each of the other two stages in this stage of play. This is where we get to feel what it would be like to *be* someone else, how it would feel for us to be in their life. This is a great way to refine our imaginative and empathic skills. The world of pretending to be someone else is precisely how we develop empathy and nurture our creative capacity.

How do I re-experience this type of play now in adulthood?
The term 'role play' can send a shiver down most adults' spines after one too many training-day experiential activities. But when done playfully, the art of pretending to be someone else in some other situation can be fun and exciting (I promise).

- Drama: If drama and acting was something you enjoyed as a child, find your local community drama society and sign up to get involved. There are lots of ways of getting involved that don't mean you will be on stage in a role, but simply being around other adults who enjoy role play can be of benefit for us.

- Make a call: Have a two-sided conversation all by yourself. Hold a child's phone (or hold your stretched index finger and thumb to your ear in the style of a phone or hold a banana to ear/mouth in guise of a phone) and imagine it has just rang and you say 'Hello?' From here you get to imagine who is on the other end and what they might be saying, and you react accordingly. Another way to do this (if you have a play partner who will enter into this one with you) is to make a phone out of two paper cups/tin cans and a piece of string between them. Stand a distance that enables you to stretch both ends so the string is pulled taut. Have a playful phone call between you that starts with 'Wait until you hear what happened' as it can set a dramatic tone to have a starter phrase.

- Charades: This is a great way to structure your role play as an adult. You will need a few people and by having teams you can increase some challenge by setting timers to see who can get through as many roles as possible in a set amount of time, or simply keep score. Write a list of roles or personas on paper, put them in a bowl and take turns enacting each in the hopes that the others can guess who or what you are playing at being.

- Whodunit: Invite a group of friends over and assign roles to everyone. Then simply provide some fun props when they arrive rather than ask for full costume (unless your friends would get really into the costume idea). Each is handed a character card when they arrive and must play out the character on it with associated props. Someone is GUILTY (of what you don't know or can make up) and over the course of your evening, with everyone remaining in character you must try to discover the guilty party.

It is only by working through each of these stages that we become better able to develop the all-important capacity to self-regulate our own emotional arousal. It is never too late to re-experience these stages of play, and actually it is really important that we keep playing like this throughout our lives. If you have identified any gaps in your stages of play or if you grew up in a family where play was not nurtured or encouraged, the ideas above could serve as a play road-map to close those gaps for yourself, even now as an adult.

When we can self-regulate our emotions, we are better able to make judgements around risk and to distinguish between what is healthy or unhealthy risk-taking behaviour for ourselves. Do you know how you engage with risk? Are you a risk-taker or a risk-avoider? What would the people who know you best say about you in response to that question?

A RISK SELF-AUDIT

Take some time to stop and reflect on your own relationship with risk. Are you more driven and motivated by reward or punishment? (Note that this is not in any way intended to be a psychological measure or assessment tool – it is purely for personal and self-reflective use.)

1. Do you feel strongly motivated by money?
2. Is it difficult for you to send a meal back or make a complaint in a restaurant?

3. If you think that something is against the rules, does it stop you doing it?

4. Does alcohol feature strongly in your social life?

5. Has a hangover ever prevented you from engaging in your planned weekend activities?

6. Does how others might think/feel about you influence your actions?

7. Are you anxious or fearful in new situations? Would this cause you to withdraw from an activity/event?

8. Do you often do things to elicit praise from others, even if it is something you don't want to do?

9. If something carries an equal measure of pleasure and potential harm, would you do it?

10. How would those who know you best describe you in terms of risk – a risk-taker or a risk-avoider?

11. When you were a child did you enjoy team sports? Meeting new people?

12. Do you often suggest new things to do or new ways of doing something?

13. Can you easily list three positive risk-taking behaviours and three negative risk-taking behaviours?

14. What kind of risks did you take when you were a teenager? Were you the instigator of these behaviours or a follower when someone else suggested them?

15. Have you ever shoplifted? How did it feel before/during/afterwards?

16. Have you ever been arrested? How did it feel for you? What happened afterwards?

17. Do you find it easy to speak in public?

18. Is it easy for you to ask for a raise at work?

19. How do you feel when you see children/other people fall and hurt themselves? What do you do/say?

20. How do you feel/behave when attending sports/activities?

As children, play helps us to develop and manage risk-taking behaviour in our lives. Remember the first time you free-wheeled down a steep hill on your bike, that fear and excitement blending wildly inside your body, and then you turned a corner or hit the brakes too hard too fast and came off the bike. That was risk-taking play that taught you an important lesson about self-regulation.

Beyond this overt risk-taking play, risk plays an active role in lots of ways we play. When we invited another child into our play, we were taking a risk as to what they would introduce to the play, how it would change the game and how we felt within the play.

Play affords us the opportunity to make choices and decisions, some that will work out well and some that won't, and we get to learn from both. Play is a positive risk-taking behaviour/activity that strengthens and enhances our general life skills and capacity to regulate our thoughts and feelings.

Through repeated experiences of this positive risk-taking we are able to nurture our developing sense of self and inner-working model (our self-image) as well as strengthen our self-esteem and efficacy.

Risky play (and *all* play is inherently risky at varying levels) gifts us the confidence to try new things, interact with new people and put ourselves out there for new experiences while being able to regulate our thoughts and feelings about doing so. These are the life skills we need throughout our adulthood, both in work and in personal interactions. I said earlier that it needs to feel safe to play, but it also needs to feel safe to take risks.

We need to know that we have supports around us that will encourage our efforts, cheer us on as we try new things and gift us the belief that we can. A safe environment, a safe relationship, is not one that avoids challenge. Often it is because our environments and relationships feel safe that we can work through challenges and embrace challenge as an exciting opportunity. Risky play builds our confidence, both as children *and* now as adults.

Understanding your own relationship to risk-taking behaviour is really helpful when it comes to understanding some of the life choices you make. If you are risk avoidant, consider who else in your family is similar. Did you grow up with a risk-avoidant parent who urged caution and stopped you trying things that carried any level of risk in them? Or if you are a big risk-taker without consideration of consequences, consider how your parents may have influenced you in this regard. How were you encouraged and praised for risk-taking behaviour or did anyone even notice the risks you were taking? Might there have been the secondary gain of using risk-taking behaviour to be really seen and noticed by your parents? As children, we needed to take risks in unfamiliar situations and environments. We needed opportunities to try something new, even though we could not predict the outcome ahead of time and even though failure was a possibility. We needed to participate in team activities and sports where there was an in-built, inherent chance of winning and losing. We needed to be safely exposed to risks that were, at least mostly, positive risks rather than harmful, negative ones.

Was this your experience growing up? How did your parents model risk-taking with and for you? Do you see any correlation now with how you engage in risk-taking behaviour now in your life? Would you like to see this change and, if so, in what way?

Throughout our lives, we have to embrace risk, embrace failing as much as succeeding and speak about what failing teaches us. Being avoidant of risk is not the positive alternative to taking risks. Being avoidant reinforces fear and self-doubt that will impose limits on how we get to engage in and fully enjoy all that life can offer us. It can keep us in a job or relationship in our life that is not good for us but the fear of not knowing what would happen without it can paralyse us into staying there regardless. If this is you and you are fearful and thus avoidant of risk, you must gently yet firmly find opportunities to practise small risk-taking behaviour and gradually build this up. Conversely, if you are a reward-driven, impulsive risk-taker who shows little to no regard for outcomes or consequences, you will equally want to step in and modify your relationship to risk. You can do this by ensuring plenty of opportunity for safer, lower-level risk-taking and consciously hit your internal *pause* button before you act.

Healthy risk is about balance. Healthy risk is enough fear to cause us to pause and consider the consequences but enough of a reward drive for us to see that the risk is worth engaging with because of what *might* happen, and respecting what we will learn regardless of outcome.

Self-protection is one of our most basic instincts. But this instinct should inform rather than impede how we live our lives. Reasonable levels of risk should not make us feel threatened. Reasonable risk is where the potential for harm is not greater than the potential for success and benefits. It is about risk management. When children and teenagers are engaging with risk, they lack the brain development to always be able to adequately assess risk so they need the adults in their lives to manage the level of risk they are taking. Remember that the part of our brain that regulates risk-taking is underdeveloped until our mid to late twenties. Playful engagement of risk-taking behaviour is a major part of our adult development just as much as when we were children. Pause now and consider how your parents encouraged or dissuaded you from taking risks as you grew up.

- Were you encouraged to try new things?
- How did your parents encourage you to find and use your voice in groups of people? Were you encouraged to speak up or was it more *be seen and not heard*?
- Were your parents more focused on the efforts you made or the outcome/result?
- Did your parents speak with you about sex, drugs, alcohol? Do you recall *how* they spoke about such things? Was it about engaging in a positive, healthy way and staying safe or was it to avoid it with dramatic consequences if you did not? How did this affect you?
- How were you incentivised to push yourself a little beyond your limits?
- Were you allowed to take everyday risks in childhood such as climbing trees/climbing frames, learning to skate or skateboard, using cooking utensils such as knives and the oven in preparing food?
- Would you describe your parents as risk-takers or risk-avoiders?
- How was your risk-taking in adolescence (e.g. experimenting with alcohol, new looks with changing hair colour, piercings, new friends, having a relationship, lying about where you were)?

Reasonable risk-taking needs to be an active and ongoing part of our lives from the earliest ages. We need parents who can encourage appropriate risk-taking behaviour in us and lead by positive example in terms of how they engage in risk-taking behaviour themselves.

- Did you ever see your parents engaging in risk-taking behaviour? Was it mostly positive risks or negative risks?

- Did your parents try new things for themselves such as participating in group activities or sports, putting themselves in situations to meet new people, taking up a new interest and learning a new skill, speaking in front of large groups? Do you recall them preparing or talking about how these things made them feel (before, afterwards)?

- Did you ever see your parents when they were drunk (beyond tipsy)? Do you recall how their behaviour changed while drunk? How did that made you feel?

- Was your parent ever too hungover to bring you to your weekend activities?

- Do you believe that you grew up in a safe environment and that your family members were a safe/secure base for you?

- Did it feel safe to take risks in your family when you were growing up? What about now?

Even now, in adulthood, consider how risk-taking is negotiated in your life and within that of your family members. Even siblings can manifest the impact of growing up in a high risk-taking family or risk-averse family in very different ways. Are you motivated to:

- put yourself forward for promotion in work
- negotiate salary rise or more positive work conditions
- take up a new hobby/interest
- address a challenging situation with a friend/partner even if it might provoke a row or disagreement?

Do you believe that you have a comfortable relationship with things (listed below) that can be associated with more negative risk-taking behaviour?

- Alcohol: Do you find that when consuming alcohol that you drink to excess more often than not? Do you drink more than is advised on a regular basis? Does consuming alcohol change your behaviour in negative ways? Have friends ever raised your behaviour with you? Have you ever had to call in sick to work because of a hangover?

- Sex: Is sex a healthy and positive part of your life? Do you use sex in a destructive way (unhealthy relationships, unsafe sexual practice, as a substitute for emotional connection in your life)? Do your sexual choices leave you feeling positive and empowered or in a more negative state of mind afterwards?

- Drugs: Do you use drugs? If so, is your use social/recreational or a more dependent engagement? Would you consider your drug use regular (at least weekly) or sporadic (once in a while, no time pattern)? Is there a particular friend (group) with whom you engage in drug use? Would you engage with this friend or group sober? Does your drug use interfere in other areas of your life or interrupt your engagement with people/activities?

- Money: Are you responsible with money? Would those who know you best describe you as responsible with money? Do you feel that you have enough money to flow freely in/out of your life (i.e. to cover what you need to live your life and enable a fully lived and enjoyed life)? (When money does flow freely in/out of our lives it means that we earn enough money to cover overheads but also that we are not afraid to spend money on things we enjoy. It is about a balance.) Have you ever spent money on *a want* at the cost of being able to cover *a need*? Would you often do this?

In adolescence, our nucleus accumbens, the part of the brain associated with thrill-seeking and reward-driven behaviour, is developing very quickly. The part of our brains associated with judgement, inhibition control, decision-making and emotional regulation (including cause/effect thinking) – the pre-frontal cortex – is still developing right up to our mid and even late twenties. We are neurologically wired to engage in risk-taking behaviour in childhood and especially adolescence because of how our brains are developing.

Our exposure to risk should be a mostly positive experience where mastery over a task is encouraged and our effort to engage matters more than the outcome. For those of us who grew up in safe and secure environments, it most likely felt safe to take a risk knowing that we were supported regardless of the outcome (and when a situation got out of control, we knew that we could call someone to come and help us because we knew our relationship was stronger than the row this would cause).

But if you grew up in an unsafe environment, where a parent was often drunk or high, where there wasn't enough food, where money was scarce and there wasn't enough money to cover living costs or you had to move a lot or spent time living in homelessness or perhaps where there were other forms of abuse so that there was the absence of a safe, trusted reliable adult who could ensure that you were safe from harm, it may never have felt as if risk was a safe or positive thing. In your life, perhaps there was only negative risks or the negative *far* outweighed the positive. If this has been your experience, I am so sorry that you endured this. Know that you deserve good-quality care and please reach out to appropriate services to give you access to psychological and psychotherapeutic supports to process all of that. You matter and are deserving of good care – you were then and you are now. Growing up in a high-risk environment will have impacted how you engage in or avoid risk in your life now. But change is always possible – not always easy but always possible – and the tools in this book are a practical and meaningful way to begin that process of change for yourself.

HEALTHY CONNECTIONS = HEALTHY RELATIONSHIPS

The people around us are some of the most powerful influences on our autonomic nervous system. For better or worse, our relationships with the people in our lives, our engagement in our communities (participating in groups, activities, etc.) affect how we think, feel and act. When this is a positive influence, we feel safe, grounded and regulated within ourselves and thereby safe and secure enough to take risks and chances on new people and new experiences within our lives. If this has been a more negative influence though, the absence of that positive connection can leave us feeling untethered in our lives because it doesn't feel safe or secure now, just as it didn't back then.

Healthy connection with others who help keep us grounded, balanced and regulated is necessary in order to feel internally safe and secure, not just externally safe and secure. Without it, we go about our lives with a constant, even low-level, internal alarm bell ringing and that will impede the risks we are likely to take and thereby the opportunity for new, positive and healthy life-enhancing experiences.

Biological and psychological factors have significant influence on our autonomic nervous system but so too do social factors. Social marginalisation, isolation, loneliness, poverty, homelessness and a general absence of adequate social supports can all activate that internal alarm system, pushing into our survival response (either heightened, frenetic activation or immobilised shutdown). If we are in this state of survival activation for prolonged periods of time without access to a safe and co-regulating relationship (e.g. a mental-health professional) we can experience symptoms of anxiety, depression, post-traumatic stress disorder, immune disorders and physical ill-health.

Developing healthy, safe, playful and caring relationships with people who let you know that you are seen, heard, understood, accepted and loved is essential. This is important in all of our lives but is essential for trauma recovery and repairing a ruptured relationship base.

This safe relationship might be with a mental health professional first, so that it can then be experienced with someone else. Even brief social connected interactions can have positive effects on our capacity to develop and sustain healthy connections and relationships.

People in your community you can experience a casual but pleasurable (regular) connection with can include the following:

- Barista: Nothing like someone knowing your coffee order before you say it. It lets you know that you are held in someone's mind.
- Gym coach: Someone who can encourage you, praise your efforts, push you a little beyond your comfort zone in a safe, supervised way and whose reflections of you make you feel confident and competent is a great boost to self-esteem and belonging.
- Librarian: Joining your local library and going in each week allows you to build up a warm, familiar connection with the librarian who will quickly get to know you, your reading tastes and what interests and excites you.
- Hairdresser/barber: Booking into the same salon with the same stylist each time will allow you to make a connection with someone who is providing nurturing touch, who is motivated to make you look and feel good about yourself and will reflect that you do look good back to you.
- Shop-owner: Large supermarkets can be a more anonymous experience but making a casual connection with

the owner of your local small shop, where you can go in for newspapers or a few top-up shopping bits during the week is a great way to practise casual conversation and brief encounters in a safe way.

This is not an exhaustive list. You can add your own to it, such as doctor, therapist, work colleague, vet, online social-media group and any others.

THE CONTAINING FEELING OF CO-REGULATION

Co-regulation is our route to self-regulation. Long before we can 'calm down' or settle ourselves, we are calmed through others – our available and loving caregivers. We need our attachment figures to be our calm so that we can learn to calm. It takes the entirety of early childhood to develop reliable, consistent self-regulation capacity. Indeed, it is by going through the three stages of play detailed earlier that we develop our capacity for self-regulation, but even when we can self-regulate, we never lose our need to have connections with safe, trusted co-regulating others in our lives.

Co-regulation occurs when we attune or connect with another person. We experience our internal emotional state shift to resonate more in line with that person's internal emotional state. In this safe, connected state, we can experience an emotional exhale that enables repair and recovery for our autonomic nervous system, which in turn gives us physical relief.

Needing this kind of connection doesn't mean that we are needy people – far from it. As humans, we are wired for connection with others. The most healthily self-regulating people you know can only sustain their healthy self-regulation by having these co-regulating others in their lives too. It is not a weakness, and being able to develop and sustain these relationships in our lives is in fact a strength.

None of us can reach our potential alone or within systems (family or societal) that isolate, denigrate or marginalise us. We need supportive social connections and relationships with people and within our communities. We need it for our emotional and physical health and well-being. When we have grown up with it, we have a template for what we are looking for. When we have not, we need support to identify and establish this healthier template to stop us repeating unhealthy patterns of disconnection in our lives. This is why we start with small, safe, playful risk and gradually build up this capacity and openness within us.

Remember, we want to use this type of play to support and build our confidence and self-esteem, to convey that all-important sense of *wow, look at all I can do* and *it is exciting to put myself out there and take a chance on something*. Positive risk-taking fuels a strong sense of agency. Having 'agency' means that we can learn to act independently and take responsibility for our own actions while making our own free choices. It allows us to develop self-esteem, a stronger sense of self (understanding who we are in the world and in relation to the people around us) and emotional well-being. Being able to make choices and decisions for ourselves ensures that we can feel that we can influence events that affect us, develop healthy connections with others and have a positive effect on the world we live in. It ensures that we can view ourselves as competent and contributing members of society. It is certainly worth taking a risk on risk.

PLAY BREAK

Take a risk on being someone else with this simple little exercise to stimulate your imagination and therefore playful mindset. In this activity, you are going to change who you are for the length of time it takes to order a cup of coffee. You might want to try this one out at a cafe where you are not known.

Who am I?

Walk into the cafe and as you do, adopt a new persona. Give yourself a new name (it might be one of those places where they like to write your name on the coffee cup so make it a fun name – fun to say and fun to hear). Adopt a new kind of walk and physical posture. You can even give yourself a bit of a back story to really take this to another level and deepen the experience for yourself. For the length of time it takes you to queue, order, pay for and collect your coffee, *this* is the person you must be.

This activity affords you the opportunity to safely and playfully push your personal boundaries and take a risk on doing/saying/behaving in a way that may not feel entirely comfortable as 'you' but might as 'this person'.

TAKE A WALK ON THE DARK SIDE OF PLAY

Playfully engaging with dark themes can help us to develop a mastery over tension-rousing experiences.

There are dark and light aspects to our life, and there are dark and light aspects to play. Play enables a fully lived life. It is important that we can playfully engage with even dark themes in our lives, such as grief, stress, anger, rage, frustration, betrayal and fear, because it helps us to connect with those more icky and uncomfortable parts of ourselves and life that we might otherwise seek to avoid, deny, minimise or dismiss.

The experience of playing connects us with and mobilises a full range of thoughts and feelings, not just those we feel good about. This is intended to equip us to deal with challenges and conflict throughout our lives in a creative, critically considered and solution-focused way. Play relieves stress while strengthening connection (that is connection within ourselves and with others and within our environments). This is because play, even when playing with dark material, is enjoyable, and this pleasurable feeling releases endorphins that actively lower stress and help to counteract those more negative feelings.

Have you ever noticed a child at imaginative play? You will have observed everything from alien invasions, zombie uprisings, meteor attacks, characters dying and then resurrecting and sometimes all while at a family picnic in the park. Children are not afraid to play with dark themes, and such themes are nothing to be afraid of; far from it, we should welcome this dark side to play and recognise that it has as much value as the mirth the lighter side to play brings.

Themes of death, fear, loss, threat, violence and transformation permeate through children's books and indeed through most Disney cartoons (especially the earlier ones). In adult life, perhaps we seek to repeat some of these same bodily and emotional sensations by immersing ourselves in trauma-laden literature, true-crime podcasts or shows or watching horror movies. I read some dark books when I was a young teenager, books I was, in hindsight, too young to read, but I *loved* reading them, perhaps especially because I knew I shouldn't be. Reading everything Virginia Andrews ever wrote by 14 years old opened up a realm of trauma that I could simultaneously be a part of and yet apart from.

Similarly, when I watch a horror movie and I experience the assault on my senses, my heart rate increases, my breath is laboured, my eyes widen and my muscles tense, and I am poised to react for the duration of the movie. Exposure to dark content allows us to engage with darkness in the world from a comfortable distance. In this way, books and TV/movies offer a safe way to be scared. It is happening elsewhere to others but you are along for the emotional ride.

Being afraid but knowing it will be okay is powerful not only for children but for all of us. In part, it helps us to learn that we can master tension-rousing experiences and that we can self-regulate out of a state of heightened fear/emotional arousal. In other words, we learn that we can cope with being scared, more scared that we perhaps imagined we could cope with, and there is a sense of satisfaction in this realisation. We get to experience being very close to danger and dangerous people without actual risk to ourselves. There is some excitement in that experience too because these are thoughts, feelings and bodily sensations that are outside of our everyday or usual experiences. This allows us to release our darkest thoughts, feelings and urges in a safe and boundaried way.

There is also a hormonal aspect to why we can enjoy being scared. We get a surge in endorphins immediately following a fright/scare. Endorphins are our feel-good chemical. The key here is that this kind of fear can only be pleasurable because we *know* that we are safe. Without safety, it is just fear, and that is not pleasurable.

This can also be seen in how we seek to playfully scare and frighten each other. I am thinking of those 'games' whereby we hide only to jump out unexpectedly when someone else walks by, causing them to yelp and jump in unexpected fright. When we seek to scare others in play, we are exploring what it is like to be the perpetrator of fear – we get to play with power, control and dominance over others. This play offers a safe (even joyous if you both laugh about the scare afterwards) way to connect with our darker impulses.

PLAY NICELY

Do you ever recall being cautioned to 'play nicely' as a child? What did you understand by this phrase? What limits did it impose on your play?

Let's explore how play can create conflict and why this might be a good thing. Playing with themes of conflict and experiencing conflict within a playful experience can serve as a means of challenging systems of control. *Hey, that's not fair, you cheated! It's my ball, I'm going home! I'm not your friend anymore! I'm telling on you!* Sound familiar? These expressions of conflict allow us to experience a relational rupture between us and our playmate, typically followed by a relational repair when the play is altered and a new option is proffered in the interests of progressing the play beyond the conflict.

Refusing to play or refusing to follow a set of 'rules' within the play is actually an act of playfulness in itself. We have to invite both refusal and engagement within the realm of play and remember that openness to play and refusal of play are not necessarily opposites in this context. We have to feel safe to refuse to begin with, and the act of refusal can itself construct something new within the play. It is not just about saying 'no' but perhaps about communicating 'no, but...' and suggesting a change within the play. This is the importance of the darker side to play where play acts as a release of powerful energy. One minute we are laughing and hugging each other and then next someone is bleeding/crying while someone else is raging. There are valuable life skills for children in experiencing conflict in their play.

Children play out important themes such as good/evil, right/wrong through darker themes in their play. They do battle, brandish (imagined) weapons, they arrest, lock up and kidnap as part of this play. In this play, children are pushing boundaries, wondering what it would be like to be so big and powerful and bad in the world. This doesn't mean they are plotting evil deeds for the real world; this is play where anything is possible. This is also where children can see the baddie caught, held accountable, develop remorse and make repair. They can push the boundaries without crashing through them. Denying them the opportunity to play with the darker themes is denying the opportunity to see that evil can be overcome and that people are held accountable for wrong-doing.

In truth, there is no right way to play. Policing play is an intrusion and denies us the opportunity to play out internal psychic processes in a safe and creative way.

A JOURNEY THROUGH THE ENCHANTED WOODS

Fairy tales began as myths and evolved over the years. In 1813 (in a letter to the German Romantic poet, Achim von Arnim), Jacob Grimm wrote that he 'did not write the [Grimm Brothers] storybook for children, although I rejoice that it is welcome to them; but I would have worked over it with pleasure if I had not believed that it might appear and be important for poetry, mythology and history to the most serious and elderly people'. The original Grimm Brothers' fairy tales were intended to be read by adults before they were ever intended for children.

Bruno Bettelheim is a psychoanalyst who wrote one of the best-known analyses of fairy tales called *The Uses of Enchantment*. He wrote of the forest and how it is used in fairy tales to symbolise 'the place in which inner darkness is confronted and worked through; where uncertainty is resolved about who one is and where one starts to understand who one wants to be'. In most fairy tales, the character ventures into the forest and faces great darkness, threat and challenge only to emerge from the forest changed, with a new perspective on the world and greater autonomy than when they went in. The darkness of the forest proves itself to be a vital place to grow, but of course you must be able to find your way out for that growth to be affected. This is why darkness and lightness in life are important to our growth and development as people.

When (re)connecting with your own playfulness, books and stories are a great point of entry. I would strongly suggest reflecting on some of the books you loved reading as a child and rereading those now.[3]

Try this fear-mastery activity. You will need paper and markers. If you want you can add in some textured pieces (pipe cleaners/pom-poms/glitter, etc.) that you will find in a craft set.

You are going to make a monster out of things that scare you. Maybe it has a spider's head and unread emails as legs, or perhaps it is a combination of a clown's head with spider legs and a screengrab of a Zoom or Microsoft Teams room as the body. Maybe it is your first class teacher with a dog's tail and a

---

3   I have included some books in the resource list to support you in reflecting on your favourite stories and their meanings.

rat's nose. Take a few things that have scared you in your life, perhaps still scare you, and playfully arrange them into a monster of your own design. Now explore ways that you can make the monster silly. Add a hat, a red nose, draw coloured socks or high-heeled shoes onto those spider legs or a moustache on the face of your teacher or the spider. Accessorise to less-terrorise!

People sometimes ask me if I ever feel too fed up, frustrated, melancholic or anxious to play. Of course – there are times when I absolutely feel low or irritable or just on edge, but this doesn't mean I can't play. It means *how* I play and the themes in my play might well tend towards the darker side of play and that is what I invite you to do now.

Let's try a quick exercise in creativity that can be engaged with in different ways depending on your emotional state entering into it.

POETRY SALAD

Write something using the following words, in any order you choose and noting that each word can feature a maximum of three times. You do not have to use every word. You can add personal pronouns of your choosing.

Dark – Joy – Deep – Lost – Echoes – Once – Laughter – Lonely – Curious – Heart – Through – Breath – Man

– Woman – Someone – Running – Jumping – Bells – The
– Beginning – Warmth – Always – Water – Of – To – If
– Am – Was – Is – In – And – There – My – Found –
Sound – See – Animal – Gentle – Silly – Banana – Sinking
– Feathers – It – Air

(Example A) Once I was lost in the deep dark and I was lonely. There was the sound of bells. I am running, I feel my breath. It is deep. I am found in the laughter of his curious heart. There is warmth. It is my beginning.

(Example B) In the beginning there was an animal. It was gentle and silly. It found a banana. It was running, jumping, sinking through feathers. The sound of laughter echoes in the air. There is joy, always joy.

CHAPTER THREE

Play in Our Relationships

When I wrote my first book (*15-Minute Parenting 0–7 Years*) I included a reference to play in adult relationships, play without intimate agenda, just play. I talked about mock interviewing each other while doing the dishes, telling each other jokes, sharing stories, reading each other favourite books from childhood. At the time, I remember an interviewer saying to me that while they 'got the point and purpose of this and how it would impact relationships' she cringed at the thought of doing it. Fast forward four years and here I am writing an entire book dedicated to embracing play in our adult lives.

Play is a relational experience that drives connection. If you want your relationship to be fun, pleasurable and something to be enjoyed rather than endured then we need to look at ways to bring more playfulness into that relationship. I am talking about all of our relationships, be they with intimate partners, our siblings, ageing parents, friends or our children. My 15-Minute

Parenting series really focuses on using play to strengthen our relationship as parents with each other and with our children. Here I want to broaden that out to be more encompassing of *all* our relationships. For ease of reading, I am breaking this chapter into sections that speak to our different adult relationships.

PLAY WITHIN OUR ADULT RELATIONSHIPS

Play is an essential part of what keeps us connected as adults, especially within our intimate partner relationships. But it is just as important that we have a way of playfully connecting outside the bedroom just as it is important in the bedroom too. This is really play without an intimate agenda.

When I say *play without intimate agenda,* I am seeking to separate play in adult lives from just flirtation or seduction. This is not to say that I don't think sex can and should be playful. It really should, because sex that has playfulness in it is more magical (in terms of the creativity and fantasy it evokes) and fuels deeper connections. In my work with parents and adults, I hear more and more about how their intimate life has become rushed, functional and something that feels more like a duty than the fun, pleasurable connection it once was. Life is busy, we are rushing and under pressure. It can be difficult to prioritise fun and pleasure time together... and yet, investing in this part of our intimate relationships is an investment in all other aspects of our life and general well-being.

This kind of playfulness in sex (I don't mean pausing to tell a knock-knock joke) can fuel tenderness, excitement, curiosity, joy and connection. It enables us to build our capacity to open our emotional selves up for other people and be able to feel safe, secure and held in connection with another person. The playful space of intimacy with others is the source of the *aliveness* we crave in adulthood. It is in this space that the playful teasing and messing around we are familiar with from childhood play is re-experienced in adult sexuality and intimate connection between adults. This is when play takes on a more seductive and sensual function.

A study examining adult playful individuals showed that not only do playful people have more romantic connections and not just casual flings – as one might expect with playful people who are often perceived as light-hearted and not taking life too seriously – but also more long-term relationships. The researchers found that playful traits deemed ubiquitous in young mammals were also very useful in adult life in terms of attracting a mate and even in reproduction. But also, that playfulness in adulthood can be associated with physical fitness, activity and health. It would appear that playful adults are attracted to other playful adults.

IF YOU SAY YOU ARE, YOU ARE (PLAYFUL THAT IS)

A study by Dr René Proyer (2017a) involving over 3,000 people showed that when playful people self-describe as playful, other people tended to agree and to view them as playful people.

I find this really interesting and, for me, it would follow suit that when someone believes themselves to be playful, they act in overtly playful ways. If you want to be more playful in your life, identify as playful to yourself and out loud to others because you will find evidence for this belief and thereby it is true.

In Proyer's study, four different types of play tendencies in people were found:

Other-directed playfulness – these are people who enjoy messing around with friends.

Light-hearted playfulness – these are people who view everything in life as playful.

Intellectual playfulness – these are people who tend to mostly play with ideas and thoughts.

Whimsical playfulness – these are people who show interest in quirky or unusual things and find their entertainment in the smaller more everyday type of occurrences and observations.

I don't think you can only be all one and not another, so you may find you have crossover tendencies in your playful preferences but are more dominant in one type over another. Pause and have a think about this now. It might be worth reflecting on your childhood playfulness and which type best describes you, then your adolescent playfulness, young adulthood and adulthood. Maybe you were light-heartedly playful but somewhere along life's journey, owing to experiences of one kind or another, it stopped feeling safe to view the world this way. Maybe you now realise that intellectual playfulness best describes you but you had never really considered this tendency as a form of playfulness due to how you were defining play or picturing playful people as other than you.

HOW TO GIVE IT A GO AND STRETCH YOUR PLAYFULNESS BEYOND YOUR COMFORT ZONE

Other-directed play: Tag-rugby, chasing/tag, gathering with friends and sharing laughter while recounting funny things you have jointly experienced in the past, 'horsing around' type of interaction. Try playing Twister with a couple of other adults.

Light-hearted play: Open to evolving ideas and plans in the moment, actively not taking life too seriously, deciding in the moment, 'You know what would be fun right now? Let's do…' Try accepting a last-minute invitation (or initiating one) without much of a plan – 'Would you like to meet up at X place and hang out?' – then see where the day/night takes you.

Intellectual play: This is about enjoying activities that make you think and moreover think in new ways. Try games like Sudoku, Wordle, Words with Friends, jigsaws, problem-solving puzzles, board games with strategies or even a Rubik's cube.

Whimsical play: Embracing the quirky, unusual and even bizarre as something fun and engaging. Try moving around your kitchen as a butterfly, mime that you are running for a bus without your legs moving, adopt a new unusual walk from your house to the bus stop, make up a life story for a stranger you see on public transport or walking ahead of you.

The other thing that Proyer's research showed is that we can assess playfulness in a more general way, so-called *global playfulness*, which is really about measuring or taking stock of your general demeanour as mostly playful, open to a variety of playful activities and living life with a generally high level of intensity around playfulness. I think that you can view yourself as generally playful/not very playful in general and within that space identify which of the four types detailed above you are mostly aligned with, even if it is not much of the time.

In another of his published papers, Proyer (2019) explores how each of these playful types results in different levels of relationship satisfaction *but* that overall, playful people have a higher number of romantic partners over the course of their life, both short- and long-term partners.

Play promotes intimacy, alleviates tension, strengthens communication and helps us to create meaningful connections with one another. It is the essence of adult relationships. Remember when we are talking about play, in general, not just in this context, that we are seeing play as the act of playing but also that playfulness is a state of mind – a way of being.

When we talk about play in intimate adult relationships, this could be role play as an act of play or the more playful state of mind that brings joviality, cheekiness, creativity (helps to prevent monotony), touch, jokes, (light and never nasty) teasing, open communication (which promotes shared joy and collaborative meaning-making) and connection into the relationship.

Understanding human connection, in all of its forms, and the role that play has in strengthening and enhancing this connection and in stabilising adult relationships is the way that we deepen our understanding of what is and is not working for us in our relationships.

While I do believe that playfulness of a sexual or sensual nature within intimate relationships is really important in sustaining that relationship, it is not the specific form of play that I specialise in. But if this is a specific area that you would like to delve deeper into and find out more about, I can suggest the work of sex educator Jenny Keane, who offers very playful and educational webinars and programmes on increasing pleasure, both personally and in a relationship with another person.

- Playful couples are often the happiest couples. Playful couples enjoy each other in a variety of ways *and* are enjoyed by each other in return. Any of the research into this area bears this out, showing that people who experience higher levels of playfulness within their intimate relationship tend to experience more positive feelings and thoughts about each other (and themselves) and are generally positive and satisfied within what is a generally closer relationship.
- Playfulness can be anything from sharing a joke, being light-hearted, energetic, upbeat, smiling and seeking to make the other person smile too. It is being able to have fun together and laugh at and with each other in a manner of shared joy. Being able to be silly together promotes close connection, strengthens communication and enables us to feel more relaxed with each other. Please don't panic at this point if this reads as

something that requires you to be a costume-owning role-playing, juggling comedian – it doesn't at all. It is about deepening our understanding of what it *is* to play and challenging our preconceived notions of what constitutes a playful relationship. I invite you to play with playfulness in your relationship to find what rhythm of play best suits you and your partner.

SOME WAYS TO BRING THIS TYPE OF PLAYFULNESS INTO YOUR ADULT RELATIONSHIP

First-date magic: Replicate your first date again and talk about what it was that attracted you to each other – your thoughts and feelings when you first connected.

Meet-up: Role-play meeting as though you were strangers. You can do this in lots of ways:

- Book a restaurant and be each other's blind date, arriving separately and starting with introductions.
- Arrange for one of you to go and sit in a bar and wait for the other one to arrive and approach you as a stranger, then start flirting.
- Stage a dinner at home and speak only in innuendo to each other.

- Book a hotel room and send a message to your partner to meet you there, leaving the room key at the door for them – get there early and set the mood.

Slow dance: Dancing is a great way to experience close physical intimacy along with the co-regulation of the rhythm and synchrony of music and movement. Play a slow set and ask each other to dance.

Flirt: Back-to-basics, good old-fashioned flirting. Smile and wink at each other (subtly of course, not constantly because that's just weird), have a code language to send each other subtle, sensual messages, leave notes for each other (in the car, lid of coffee jar, etc.), send flirty, provocative texts to each other during the day.

Massage each other: Touch each other. The deep pressure touch of massage is a great regulation tool. Massage lowers the stress hormone cortisol and produces/releases happy hormones like dopamine and oxytocin. The skin is the largest organ of the human body, and touch is the first sense we develop at the start of life and the last one to leave us at the end of our lives. Touch is a great way to increase intimacy, sensuality and connection, so even getting outdoors for a walk while holding hands and/or putting your arm around each other can be a nice simple way to connect with touch.

Food play: Take turns blindfolding each other and feeding each other sensual food (chocolate-covered strawberries, cherries, whipped cream – done the right way, most foods can take on a sensual feel).

Get steamy: Share a shower (add some essential oils to the steam) or bath together.

Create time for cuddles: Hug each other every day, aiming for a good 15-second embrace each time that you do. Snuggle up on the sofa to watch a movie, bring breakfast up to bed and snuggle under the duvet while you eat, chat and connect. If you have children, seek a generous relative who will babysit so you can have a night alone, be that at home or in a hotel.

Say it and mean it: Tell each other *I love you* every day, no matter what else might be going on, and be specific by adding on to this, *I love you and I really love the dimples in your cheeks when you smile/your bright blue eyes/how strong your arms feel around me when you hug me*. Pay each other meaningful compliments each day.

Fantasise: Share your intimate fantasies with each other in as much detail as you can. No judgement or inferences about what each other share. Now see if there is any fantasy or aspect of a fantasy that you can recreate together in real life.

Read to me: Read a passage from a book you are reading but do it in a sultry voice (this can also be quite funny depending on what you happen to be reading). Better still, buy some erotica and sit and read stories or passages out loud to each other, ensuring you look up and lock eyes often as you do so.

Sex toys/Sex play: Ensure that you are both very comfortable with this, and explore and discuss what might feel comfortable because even this discussion can fuel intimacy when done playfully. If this is a new area of exploration for you, maybe start with something at the gentler end of the range and remember that if it doesn't feel good, fun or pleasurable then stop and change what you are doing.

Reciprocity is the process of giving and receiving and it holds significant influence over our autonomic nervous system. Reciprocity can be experienced via communication involving talking/listening and of course in playing together. Healthy relationships tend to have higher levels of this reciprocity, meaning that each person can step up or lean in when the other might need more and can equally expect the same from the other person when they need more support based on what life throws at us. Relationships that lack reciprocity show patterns of just one person's needs always being prioritised and these relationships are draining and activate our autonomic nervous system in unhealthy ways. Ensuring your relationships are rooted in higher levels of reciprocity fuels the type of connection and co-regulation that supports us in feeling safe and authentically connected with the other person, in good times and in challenging times.

Mutual play involves high levels of reciprocity and as such is a very healthy form of play in adult relationships. Mutual play is a space where both parties can occupy a shared space without either being overwhelmed. So, when you are playing with someone else, it is great that you feel you are having fun but don't be the only one having fun – there has to be shared joy in the mutual play experience.

MUTUAL PLAY – HAVING PLAYFUL RELATIONSHIPS WITH OUR FAMILY MEMBERS

Playing together is one of the most effective tools we have to build strong relationships between people because play brings joy and resilience into relationships, which means it can also heal old resentments and hurts. Try applying this to some important but perhaps more fraught relationships in your life. It is likely that a particular relationship with a family member (sibling or even parent) will come to mind. Play supports responsive and connected relationships. Ask yourself, how playful is your relationship with your family members (the answer is likely to be different for different people) and now ask yourself if there is a family relationship you would like to begin to heal through increased playfulness.

Our siblings are our first experience of friendships and our first experience of enemies. The sibling relationship is emotionally loaded, and if you want to heal, reconnect or simply grow that relationship into something that is more like friendship in nature, step one will be to release any emotional load you are carrying over from your childhood, as you are not children anymore.

Approach your relationship with an adult sibling with a fresh perspective and be open to being surprised. Invite them to join you in something playful (a prosecco and paint class where the focus is more on the canvas than each other but you can share a laugh while you co-create some art; a salsa night where you will be moving around with partners dancing and as such it is less intense than the two of you sitting staring at each other all night; a just-for-fun sports club such as tag-rugby; a music gig where you can have dinner/drinks before or after). Strengthening a sibling relationship through play is a mutual endeavour – they have to want it too. This is why mutual play can be so effective here.

Mutual play is also a very important form of connection between adults. It offers opportunity to experience shared joy, and within this shared joy, we will experience a release of those feel-good endorphins that not only make us feel good but, in this context, make us feel good *together* and in connection with each other.

MUTUAL PLAY ACTIVITIES TO TRY IN ANY ADULT RELATIONSHIP (INTIMATE PARTNER/SIBLING/FRIEND)

Car games: While sitting in a car together play the alphabet game, whereby you pick a theme (e.g. fruit/colours/music bands/girls names) and take turns working your way through the entire alphabet one letter at a time as far as you can. For example, fruit: person (a) says apple; person (b) says banana; person (a) says cherry; person (b) says dragon fruit and so on.

You can also play 20 questions, whereby you pick someone (well known/famous) and the other person gets to ask a maximum of 20 questions that have yes/no answers to work out who it is.

Play a fun word game. Start by taking some time to come up with three to five new words that you have made up. In turns, one of you will say a word aloud while the other person tries to spell it. They can ask you to repeat the word a second time before they spell it. The person who spells the word gets to define it and based on the definition, the person whose word it was at the start now must act out the word based on the new definition.

For example:

Person (a): The word is parfle.

Person (b): Repeat it please.

Person (a): Par-fle.

Person (b): P-A-R-F-I-L?

Person (a): Almost but not quite. One more try.

Person (b): Okay, P-A-R-F-L-E?

Person (a): Yes, that's it. Now what does it mean?

Person (b): Parfle (a verb) means speaking with a full mouth while chewing at the same time.

Person (a) acts out speaking with a full mouth while chewing.

Whoever elicits the most laughter wins the game.

After the happily ever after: Take a well-known fairy tale, or even an adult book you have both read, and between you, plot out a sequel to it. What happened after the happily ever after? Take each of the characters individually and plot out their story, agreeing on any overlaps between characters. You could even introduce a couple of new ones as a sequel often introduces new characters.

You could flip this one a bit and design a prequel story for the villain or, as a bigger challenge, take one of the more minor characters and give them a meaty prequel to star in.

At the end, decide who would play each role in the movie version of your story.

Shopping challenge: Challenge each other to find a set number of items that begin with a certain letter while doing the grocery shopping or to find a set number of items of clothing in a particular colour in window displays of shops.

PLAY TO PROMOTE CONNECTION AND COMMUNICATION

Partner pull-up: Sit on the floor, facing each other and within arm's reach. Sit on your bottom with your knees pulled up and ensure your toes are touching each other's. Reach out and hold each other's hands, sustaining eye contact. Now lean back away from each other while pulling yourselves upwards. Ideally you will manage to pull each other up from sitting to standing. Sometimes you won't and you will collapse down but that is fun too! Keep trying until you get it – once standing, try a double high-five clap or, better still, a hug.

Describe and draw: Sit facing away from each other, perhaps place two chairs back-to-back for this. One of you has paper and a pencil (and something to lean the paper on). The other person picks a household object to describe. You will ideally hold the object so that you can describe it in as much detail as possible *without* naming what it actually is. Based on your clear, detailed description, your partner should be able to draw/identify the object you are describing. Switch roles and repeat this one at the end.

As a little note on this one: this is a fun activity that can be played over video call if you are separated by distance and still want to playfully connect.

Arm/thumb/leg wrestling: You may well be familiar with the concept of arm wrestling and thumb wrestling but perhaps not leg wrestling. This is going to seem a little out there *but* that is why I am suggesting three variations so you can find the one that suits you – don't start with leg wrestling; maybe build up to it. For leg wrestling, two people lie flat on their backs on the floor in opposite directions so that each one has their head at approximately the level of the other person's hip. They lock arms. Each person raises up their inside leg (the one closest to each other) three times, tapping each other's foot in a 1, 2, 3, GO motion. Then you each wrap your leg around the other person's leg and try to flip them over. This

is a lot of fun, though of course don't do this option if you
are carrying a back injury.

Paper airplanes: Write a message (playful or intimate) on a
piece of paper and then turn it into a paper airplane to send
over to your friend/partner. They can read and write their
own to send back to you. This is one you can make even more
playful with a few extra people. Everyone writes a message and
makes a paper airplane or two. Drop them into a bag then
tip them all onto the floor. Each person picks up a couple of
planes and you fly them between you all at the same time.
Whatever one(s) you catch are your messages and after reading
them you have to try to guess who sent them.

A teenager I worked with once told me about a cool way to
make non-paper airplanes that they had learned when in the
Scouts. They used other household items to transform into
an airplane, the challenge being that it had to fly across the
room to be successful. We did this using tinfoil, cereal-box
cardboard but the really new one for me was taking a cloth
(like a dishcloth more than a facecloth), wetting it, freezing
it and folding the frozen material into an airplane to see if
it would hold long enough to fly. What other non-paper
airplane materials can you think of? Why not try some of
these out together?

Take care to care: Nurture play is really important in strengthening connection. For this one you will need a cotton ball. That's it, just a cotton ball. Over the years of running play workshops and training programmes as well as my clinical work, I have met countless people who really dislike the sensation of cotton wool so if this is you, simply switch to a soft-headed make-up brush (like an eyeshadow blender or blusher brush) or a soft-headed paintbrush.

Invite your play partner to close their eyes and without peeking they simply name the part you are touching. Gently (but firmly enough that they feel it and not so light that it is tickly on the skin) touch their forehead, eyes, cheeks, nose, lips, chin, ears, hands, neck… anywhere that you can see without going under clothes.

After a couple of minutes of that, tell your partner that all they have to do is keep their eyes closed and feel the touch without naming where it is. Now you will give them a full-face massage with the cotton ball or the brush, using enough pressure that they feel it, without it being too heavy or too light of touch. Go all round their face, tracing across the forehead, around the cheeks, down the nose, gently over the eyes and lips. Do a few laps of their face.

With both activities, be aware of how their body and facial muscles relax as the activity progresses and their breathing deepens and slows down. If their body stays tense or becomes increasingly tense and you observe tense breathing patterns or scrunched facial muscles, notice this and let the person know that you see they are not comfortable and invite them to open their eyes and to show you on your hand the type of touch that feels more comfortable to them.

This should feel relaxing and comfortable. If you would rather not have the person touch your face, that is okay. Offer your outstretched hand or rest your hand on their knee or your own knee, again depending on what is most comfortable for you. You could roll up your sleeves and refocus the activity on your arms, from your elbow to your fingertips.

Weather report: This is a playful massage activity. Sit in front of each other with one of you turning your back in front of the other. The person sitting behind will do a touch-based weather report on the back of the other person and then you will swap around so that you give and receive from each other as part of this activity.

Rain – drum on their back with your fingertips on both hands.

Thunder – using the edge of both hands, make a chopping motion over their back.

Clouds – using both hands in a dough-squeezing motion, make clouds around their back.

Wind – sweep your hands over/back from one side of their back to the other.

Sun – using the palm of one hand, make big sun circles all around their back.

In general, use the kind of pressure described above but ask the receiver what type of touch feels best for them and adjust accordingly. Name the weather as you go: 'It's raining and raining and then you hear thunder in the distance and getting louder as it gets closer. The clouds sweep in over the sky and the wind builds up. But then the sun comes out and clears the clouds, ensuring no more wind or rain or thunder, just nice warm sun.' At the end, I always ask the person what their favourite weather was and will end with a little extra of that type of touch.

There are lots of ways to play in this mutual shared way with another person in your life. You may find that some of these activities bring one person to mind more than another and that is because you know the relationships in your life and you know who is likely to respond best to each activity. Trust your play instinct and invite that person to play with you. If the other person seems sceptical or wary of what you are suggesting, blame the book! Tell them that you are reading this book that talks about how good it is for adults to play more and you want to try some of the ideas out so that it sounds as if they are doing you a favour by playing along – once play is made possible and inviting, full playful engagement will follow.

FINDING FRIENDS IN ADULTHOOD

I have mentioned the term 'play partner' in a number of the activities in this book. Who that play partner is will differ for each of us. For many of us it will be a friend. But in adulthood, meeting and making new friends can be very challenging. This may be, in part, because you have always found making new friends difficult throughout childhood and adolescence, but it can also be that this is quite a new experience for you. Friendships are a very different kind of relationship to family ones because we *choose* our friends. Because friendship is a voluntary relationship, it can suffer when competing with the relationships we have set obligations to (family, partner, children). It is easier to cancel a catch-up with a friend than it is to let down an ageing parent or miss a family event. It doesn't mean you don't care about your friend.

Friendships get de-prioritised as we grow up, yet these are the relationships we crave and miss when it is absent.

I asked a question on my social media. *Do you find it hard to meet/make new friends in adulthood?* The results were fascinating and many people added detailed comments beyond the simple yes/no question box I had posted. Across platforms, the average was 71% of people who found it hard to meet/make new friends in adulthood. Some people I spoke with talked about how new friendships in adulthood tend to centre around purpose such as becoming friends with parents of kids in your own child's class at school or with someone who is involved in a community activity with you. Others talked about it being easier to make new casual friendships in adulthood rather than deeper connections with new friends, as adults seem more guarded about new people entering their lives. A few more people spoke to me about a sadness when old friendships change and you don't quite feel the same connection you did when you were younger.

WHY DO WE FIND IT DIFFICULT TO MAKE NEW FRIENDS IN ADULTHOOD?

Loneliness is one of the biggest contributors to mental ill-health in adulthood. How we experience loneliness will vary greatly as everyone's experience of it differs. Loneliness occurs when our desire and even overt attempts at forging social and emotional connection with others are not reciprocated. Loneliness itself is not a mental-health condition but it is strongly associated with many mental illnesses such as depression and anxiety. It can also deeply affect our self-esteem and impact our sleep patterns.

It is rarely spoken about in this context but as discussed in the section on risk, isolation can trigger our internal survival responses. The pandemic has exacerbated loneliness for many. This is especially true for adults who live alone. Access to social outlets such as the gym, the office, the pub, restaurants, even to each other's houses was extremely restricted, so efforts to stay playfully engaged with our friends and family moved into the virtual world. Maybe you tried to learn a new instrument or crack how to paint a masterpiece with YouTube tutorials, and who among us didn't try online karaoke and quizzes as a way of linking in with our friends? As time went on though, even the most socially engaged and outgoing of us found ourselves floundering when faced with yet another Zoom quiz night. Many of us will have found that our time online engaging in social-media connections increased as we searched for that sense of belonging and connection we were no longer getting through in-person interactions. Technology can and does have a myriad of social benefits as we all experienced over this same pandemic period. It enabled us to work from home, to stay in touch with friends and family we could not see and to feel connected in a time of disconnect.

Online, virtual connections can be a great short-term substitute but cannot replace in-person, subjective, interpersonal connection. Being with someone in the same space, in close physical proximity, locking eyes, turned in towards each other, experiencing the co-regulation of matched affect in moments-of-meeting and experiencing shared joy is essential in our lives. As such, symptoms of loneliness and associated mental-health challenges are on the rise among the adult population.

For most people, in childhood you can make a friend just by going to the playground where there are other children, but there isn't really a playground setting for adults, is there? Instead, we need to find a playful space.

Our friendships evolve and change over the trajectory of our lives. It can be very difficult when one ends, regardless of the circumstances, and the idea of having to move on and find new friends can be very daunting. Sometimes it can feel frustrating; we are adults – why are we so concerned with friends? Isn't this something that children or teenagers have to deal with?

We need friends in our lives, no matter how old we are. At different stages of our lives we may have had great friends, but life moves in different directions for each of us and sometimes we outgrow our friends. This doesn't mean that those friendships didn't matter – they did, but it is healthy to develop new friendships that are in synch with new chapters of our lives. Developing and sustaining friendships takes considered effort, but the social, emotional and health benefits we gain from reciprocal friendships in our adult lives makes the investment a very worthwhile one.

GOOD FRIENDS ARE GOOD FOR YOUR HEALTH

Having friends around you means having someone you can call on to both celebrate your highs and support you during your lows and this helps to defend against feelings of isolation and loneliness in adulthood. Good friends give us an increased sense of purpose and belonging while boosting our self-esteem by making us feel wanted and relied on. We feel generally happier, and this in turn arms us with those all-important emotional and social resources to know that we can handle any stresses that come our way.

If you are lucky enough to have a long-term friend or a few such friends throughout your life, that is fantastic. This means you have grown up and moved forward in your lives together. You enhance and support each other's life choices and this is a supportive space. You can even experience that this connection endures without structure. What I mean is, the kind of friendships we have that we can go weeks, even months, without contact but as soon as we reconnect, that spark is still there and still active. Some long-term friendships can feel like hard work and take a lot more from you than they return, so you may need to pause and audit such friendships in your life.

TRUST AND KINDNESS ARE KEY TO HEALTHY FRIENDSHIPS

Trust is the basis of all healthy relationships. Perhaps this is why it can be so difficult to make new friends in adulthood. I mentioned how children just seem to 'be' friends when they meet on a playground. As adults, we have a much higher level of self-consciousness. This can bring with it the benefits of insight and self-awareness but also that heightened awareness of risk, that people may not be who they say they are. The risk of being hurt, rejected or judged is something we are much more aware of as adults, and it also takes effort to establish a level of trust in someone new.

It was easier to establish trust in other children when we were young so we can carry those friends with us into adulthood because it feels safe, familiar and comfortable, even if the nature of that friendship has changed and become more one-sided than it used to be. If a previous friendship has ended in a negative way with a break of trust, leaving us hurt, rejected or abandoned, it can be even harder again to open ourselves up to trust someone new.

It takes time to establish a new friendship in adulthood and isn't time the one resource we feel we never have enough of? Feeling that we do not have the time can prevent us pursuing a friendship – but friendship is the one thing we need to create time and space for.

Signing up to a club or organisation where you will meet people with whom you have a shared interest is worth doing because it offers instant common ground with new people, and if there are weekly meetings or training, this provides frequent and regular contact.

IF YOU CAN DO ANYTHING, DO KIND THINGS

Kindness is central to developing compassion and connection, so it is important that we invest in kindness, and one way is to playfully engage with it. We are all familiar with the internet meme *If you can be anything, be kind* and if I am honest, it is a phrase I struggle with. For me, kindness isn't simply something we are, it is something we do. It is a conscious choice to do kind things and to do them often. So rather than thinking *be kind*, think of practical ways that you can *practise kindness* daily. Kindness isn't just good for those we show it to, it is really good for us. Kindness releases dopamine and oxytocin, often called the feel-good hormones. Acts of kindness fuel connection and raise our capacity for empathy, which also drives us to connect more with other people. But it needs to start with showing ourselves the type of kindness we would so willingly give to others.

Treat yourself and show yourself the kind of kindness you would want your friend to show you. This also helps to make us more appealing as a friend to others. One way to do this is to pay yourself a daily compliment. I take my lead on this from my daughter, who each morning stands in front of the mirror and declares out loud *I look FABULOUS today*. So each morning, stand in front of the mirror and compliment yourself out loud because it is good for you and also anyone else you live with (especially if you have children) to hear you do this.

You will often hear the phrase *survival of the fittest* but survival really belongs to the most adaptable. Playful people are highly adaptable and can roll with changing situations with a greater degree of ease. Nurturing our capacity for kindness, to self and others, helps to strengthen our capacity for connection with others. Playful people tend to be kind people and vice versa because both are connection-seeking traits.

Try making a kindness list and fill it with lots of playful activities. I like to include lots of small gestures as well as a few bigger acts because the smaller gestures we can practise daily and we can build up to bigger acts less frequently. Make your list as long as you can and tick off the ones you know that you already practise, or find easy to practise, and highlight a few others you have to be more mindful about. A bigger-scale act of kindness could be a fundraiser or throwing a surprise party.

- Write out a joke and put it into someone's pocket so that they discover it after they have left your house and get a laugh from it.
- Make up a short rhyme/song to send as a voice note to someone, or call them and sing it to them.
- Go into a local nursing home to sit, talk, listen and read with a resident who may not get many visitors.
- Send someone you know a take-a-break envelope in the post (put a teabag, face mask and bar of chocolate into

an envelope and post it to a friend with a note saying 'take a break and treat yourself'.

- Video yourself reading a storybook for children and send the video to friends/family who have children.

HOW CAN I STAY CONNECTED WITH FRIENDS OR CREATE NEW CONNECTIONS EVEN WHEN I REALLY DON'T HAVE MUCH TIME?

I am going back to my 15-minute daily practice mantra here. If you can chisel out 15 minutes each day to devote to your friendships, it will pay off. Make a call, send a text, record a voice note, share a photo or a news story the other person will find interesting or amusing. Take note of nuggets of information friends give us about an important meeting, interview or event coming up for them and proactively reach out to say that you are thinking of them and hope it went well. Send some messages that don't always require or demand a response. Make suggestions to meet up, hang out and engage in a shared interest activity. If it is a friend who has young children, suggest somewhere that children can come and safely play while you sit or walk and catch up. Leave the social media for your own downtime and keep your phone in your pocket when spending time with friends. To stay interesting to others, we must also aim to be interested in what interests them.

How often do you hear or say *we must catch up soon?* In that moment, I truly think many of us mean it, but then we walk away, get caught up in the demands of everyday life and a plan never emerges from what was likely a genuine intention at the time.

BE INSPIRED BY YOUR CREATIVE AND PLAYFUL FRIENDS AND ACQUAINTANCES

On social media, audit your follow lists and ensure that you are following playful and creative people/accounts and allow them to inspire you. This way, even if you don't feel you have many creative or playful people in your life right now, you can still access inspiration with online connections.

Here are three simple steps to follow.

1. Take inspiration
2. Take action
3. Take part.

I am very lucky, as are so many of us, to know a lot of very clever, talented and creative people. I enjoy them, I enjoy their creativity and that enjoyment sparks interest in me to try my hand at activities I probably wouldn't have considered previously.

One such person is Vanessa Sinclair, a psychoanalyst and artist, writer, podcaster and generally creative individual. She published a beautiful book called *Switching Mirrors* that is a collection of poems made from what she calls the cut-up method, cutting up newspaper and magazine words and images. She calls her *Switching Mirrors* a book of *cut-up poetry* (www.chaosofthethirdmind.com). I love it so much that beyond her book and a framed piece in my home, I have started to play with this medium myself. I sit with my weekend newspaper and a Stanley knife and I slice and dice words, phrases, images and then I arrange them collage-style into something I consider beautiful or meaningful or simply nonsensical but enjoyable. I enjoy it and I wouldn't have tried this out had it not been for Vanessa's work because prior to this, my instant association with cut-up newspaper pieces was that they resembled ransom notes and nothing more. I find this to be a mindful activity that helps to anchor me to the present moment where my sole focus is on the words and phrases I am cutting out. It activates my own creativity and imagination as I rearrange those words to make something new emerge from them.

I invite you to try this one for yourself, at least once. Take this weekend's newspapers and as you flick through, stop at any word, phrase or image that really grabs your attention, even momentarily. You don't have to only take words you like – include some you dislike and basically go with any words that you have a reaction to. I find that once I start with this, other words jump out at me that might fit in or around that first one. I keep a small tin box with my paper cutter, glue stick, a collection of words and small images I spot in newspapers, a second-hand book (I like the old look to the pages and I can pick up some children's books with images there too) and old magazines. I like to have a stockpile of options when I feel like doing this activity.

Consider which creatives you enjoy following online or whose work you have always or even just recently admired. It doesn't have to be artists – it might be in the area of cooking, sport, music – but whatever it is, let what you admire inspire you, and try it out yourself. This is not about expertise – it is about experience.

WHY CASUAL ACQUAINTANCES CAN BE A GOOD THING

Some of us do perfectly well with just a few close friends who we may only see and spend infrequent time with but with whom we have an authentic connection. These can be people in our work environment, the new gym we joined, the friend of a friend we met while out one night. As we navigate our way through adulthood, the ideal may be that we stay in touch with a handful of old friends but continue to pick up some new ones along the way, some who will endure and some who won't. Sometimes a friendship is who and what we need at a particular point in our lives and when that time has passed, the friendship gradually flounders or sizzles out. No row, no drama – it was valued for what it was.

This is how adult friendship tends to work and work out best. We take available connections and craft a friendship from them – a colleague, a friend through a partner, a friend from an activity. If you are a parent, you will also cultivate some new friendships or friendly acquaintances from the parents of your kids' friends. Your children will be spending time together and it is convenient. Convenient doesn't mean it cannot also be fun, pleasurable and a nice connection... it just means the term or foundation for the friendship is different.

MAKING THE MOST OF YOUR FRIENDSHIPS

- Try to create some flexible time in your week so that you can be available on X or Y day to have a more impromptu meet-up.
- Sign up to something with a friend – a cycling club that meets every Sunday, a weekly workout class, a monthly book club.
- Be clear about what you expect from a friendship and what you expect to give to a friendship – one friend

cannot meet all of your needs; nor should we put that onto any one friend. It is more likely that you have a friend you turn to when it is advice or a quick favour you need, another you turn towards when you are up for a night out, some fun, and another is the perfect shoulder to lean on when you are in emotional crisis. Be aware of who came to mind for each when you read that and also consider who you might be for any or each of those. Be aware if you find you have a gap in any of those areas, as this is the new connection you might benefit most from.

- Be selective not collective when it comes to friendships – when time is a finite resource and friendships are a voluntary relationship we get to choose in our lives, choose wisely.

- Make online work for you – if you are seeking connections online, join group pages on topics or activities that interest you rather than mindless passive scrolling online. Share within boundaries when connecting online because while most people are genuine and who they say they are, not everyone is, so some caution is always advisable online and, as with any other relationship, if it feels intrusive or uncomfortable, shut it down. Too often, too many strangers take up too much of the finite time and space we have in our lives so apply the *selective over collective* rule of thumb in the online space too.

- Let go of a friendship that is toxic or draining you as this is not really a friendship and is taking up valuable time and space in your life that you could redirect to something and someone healthier for you.

Sometimes we will choose reconnection over new connection. Think back to a time when life was fun, you had things to do and people to do them with. Who was the friend you counted on for fun and laughter, with whom you had a close connection in your early twenties? How long is it since you spoke or saw each other? Is it worth 15 minutes of your day to reconnect with that person? Don't decide to reconnect with everyone at once. Choose one old friend with whom you haven't had much contact in some time and with whom you would like to reconnect and start there.

PLAY BREAK

Having a deep understanding of who we are better enables us to form connections with people who compliment and balance us. Try some of these activities to deepen your understanding of who and how you are (to yourself and others).

Me in a sentence: Describe yourself in five words. Then put each of those words into a sentence that describes who you are as a person. Try to imagine what five words three different people in your life would choose about you. Choose someone in your family, your closest friend and someone who only knows you as a casual acquaintance.

What I do and why: Start a sentence about what you do and continue the why in no more than ten lines below that line, each starting 'to'. It will look something like this:

I work as an accountant
to balance the books
to earn enough money
to pay the bills
to stay safe
to build a life
to share with another
to create memories
to remind us of good times
to share a laugh
to balance out life

If I could, I would: This activity is about stretching limits and pushing beyond boundaries because they don't apply here. If you could do anything, what would it be? Write five to ten of these out and you can apply some gentle structure to this by making some about you as a person, your work life, your family, your hopes and throw in a really silly, fantastical one while you are at it, just for fun.

If I could, I would take an adult gap year

If I could, I would travel to far-off places

If I could, I would change my job to become a sculptor

If I could, I would sit and have tea and cake with my parents every day

If I could, I would have a friend-and-fun day off each week

If I could, I would learn to tightrope walk

If I could, I would fly up high in the sky like a bird

If I could, I would end homelessness

Your list should see you stretch into different levels of wish fulfilment and desire. You can also apply this as a shorter, more structured activity in your daily life. Start and end your day with an *if I could, I would…* The one at the start of the day should set your intention for the day, and the one at the end of the day should reflect something you would like to change.

MENTALISATION – THE ART OF MIND PAINTING

One of the messages I have emphasised in this chapter is that play can both heal and build a relationship in our lives. It is a state of mind and a way of being. We have all experienced replaying a row in our minds or imagining what we would have liked to have done or said in a particular scenario. When we are picturing or giving imaginative quality to a story in our minds, we are mentalising. And mentalisation can be so helpful in bringing us to a place of fresh thinking and new perspective on events and relationships in our lives. For that reason, I want to introduce you to the concept and, moreover, ways that you can engage with it to strengthen and enhance playful connections in your life.

Mentalisation is the process of making sense of each other and ourselves. The concept of mentalisation is rooted in the ability to attribute a variety of mental states, such as thoughts, beliefs, desires and emotions to oneself and to others. It is an awareness that overt behaviours (what we do) are underpinned by our emotional and physical states (what and how we feel). It is a process of giving imaginative quality to information at hand; in other words, taking what little bit we know and allowing our own minds/imaginations to fill in the gaps. Because of this imaginative quality, it is also, in part, a playful process.

One of the easiest ways to understand how we do this is to, well, *do it*. Right now, as you are reading this book, I want you to simply picture the scene I am about to share with you in your mind. There is no right or wrong with this – simply allow your imagination to paint a picture or to bring this story to life for you in your mind.

Two people are seated side by side. They are silent. They
exchange a look and one gets up and walks away while the
other remains seated. The person seated takes a deep breath,
clenches their fists and starts to cry.

Pause now and slowly reread those few lines, paying close
attention to the scene that emerges in your mind as you do
so. Answer the following questions:

- Who are these people? Do they know each other? If
  so, how?
- Where are they seated? What is the physical environ-
  ment they are in?
- What is the story of what is happening?
- Consider this story from each person's perspective
- What is the dominant feeling for each person?

Now, accept that you *might be right* but you *might be wrong*. I
gave you very limited information and your imagination filled
in the blanks. You gave imaginative quality to what I told you
by picturing it in your mind using your own experiential frame
of reference. You made a series of judgements and inferences
about what was happening here that you might be right or
wrong about because that is the thing with inferences and
judgements – they are prone to error! Try doing this with
someone else, giving them the same sparse framework and

see what story they see in it. Even if you thought you were not an imaginative person, you have just imagined an entire story for two people based on minimal information. We use our imaginations in this way every day.

The key with this process, and the one I think applies across the span of our development from childhood right through to adulthood, is to *stay in a position of not knowing but seeking to better understand.* I truly believe it is the cornerstone of positive relationships – be open to being surprised by the truth.

In the theory of mentalisation, this is called adopting an *inquisitive stance.* It's akin to what I often describe as 'wondering'. When you see, hear and observe something with someone in your life, pause before you react and instead get curious and *wonder* about it. Wondering helps you to deepen your understanding of the situation, take in the perspective of the other person and perhaps anyone else involved and ensure that you respond rather than just react. Often what happens when we glean some small nugget of information is that we move very quickly to fill in the blanks of what is going on, leaping to all kinds of conclusions before landing on that *ah-ha/ gotcha* moment. No good comes from these types of *gotcha* moments. But if we are wondering, we are immediately in a more playful state of mind.

This process is about developing a capacity to put yourself in another's shoes, to be able to know how you view the situation/world while keeping another's views in mind. But this isn't some new fancy concept. You mentalise all day, every day. Children start to develop a capacity for considering another's point of view back in stage two of developmental play, at approximately four years of age, by engaging in projective/ narrative and small-world type of play.

However, when we are under high levels of stress, pressure or perhaps are dealing with a significant life event, it is quite normal to experience a temporary drop in our mentalisation levels. We may experience partial mentalisation whereby it is very difficult to put ourselves into another's perspective when we feel emotionally consumed with our own perspective and experience. At times like this, we are more likely to express certainty rather than curiosity about the thoughts of others, especially as we perceive those thoughts and feelings to relate back to ourselves. We can be rigid, concrete and literal in our thinking.

Get curious. Take this example:

Person (a): 'Oh, you haven't started the dinner yet.'

Person (b): 'Nope.' They don't look up at you but take a long slug of tea from the mug they are holding and continue to scroll on their phone.

Immediately, what is happening for person (a)? What are they thinking, feeling? What are they most likely to do or say next? What about person (b)? What is happening for them?

When we cannot hold the inquisitive stance detailed above, it is hard not to simply *react* to the behaviour in the example I just gave you. We may be running on low energy based on the experiences of our own day and we are tired, hungry and now frustrated that our partner *seemingly* is passively waiting for us to serve up dinner even though they got home first. This may bring us to start slamming drawers as we place pots and pans on the cooker, open the fridge, huffing and puffing loudly. This will either further activate the other person (who it would seem is already triggered by something) so that they say, 'I'm not hungry, I'm heading upstairs to watch TV,' or they will look up and ask, 'What's wrong with you?' Either of these is likely to further escalate you.

However, when we can hold a curiosity over certainty position, we might be able to pause and say, 'Hey, I can see you are tired (physical state) and you seem a bit fed up and frustrated (emotional state) and you decided not to bother with dinner this evening (overt behaviour). How about we get a takeaway tonight or go with a breakfast for dinner approach and just eat cereal?'

We may want to venture a link between our partner's emotional state and our own with something like, 'When I came in and saw you sitting there on your phone, the story I told myself was that you were fed up with me, that I had done something to bother you and I could feel myself getting defensive about that. That might not be your story though?'

This may afford the other person the opportunity to lean in towards you with, 'What? Goodness no, why would I be annoyed with you? I just had a tough day and am feeling really angry because...' and a new perspective can emerge without the row that the misaligned personalisation of the matter would bring.

And even when (not if, because there will be plenty of times in any close adult relationship when we do react in accordance with the story we have told ourselves that has shut off our mentalisation capacity to consider the other person's point of view) we do snap or the situation escalates to a row, we have the opportunity to initiate relational repair using the above language and approach.

Think of ways that you do repair rather than say it. Of course, you can say that you are sorry, but how do you show that you are? Maybe it's that cup of tea that you make for the other person without them asking, accompanying it with their favourite chocolate treat. Or perhaps it's the cereal or beans on toast you bring up to them as they watch TV upstairs because even though they've said they are not hungry, you know this is a comfort food they enjoy. Maybe it's a back rub or a hug or a kiss. These are actions that communicate connection. It is always easier to correct a misunderstanding from a place of emotional connection. In this stance, we are more open to another perspective or angle on the story. Without the emotional connection, we tend to adopt a defensive strategy whereby we are motivated to prove our side of the story right and are not really open to hearing the other person, as we are too busy personalising their feelings as an attack on us.

LET'S TAKE A PLAYFUL APPROACH TO REIMAGINING THE ROW

Right now, bring to mind a time when you had a disagreement with someone in your life where you believe that you were in the right and they were wrong. Once you have it in mind, recall the event in as much detail as you possibly can. Where were you, how did it start, what was the point of escalation, who said what, how did it play out and how did it end? It doesn't matter how long ago this was, once the detail is fresh in your mind right now.

Now, tell the story in as much detail as possible solely from the other person's point of view! Tell the story as if you were the other person. Don't bother to give the real account as you see it first, just immediately jump into the words and version of the event as you imagine the other person would tell it. If you can practise this with someone in your life and have them listen to you as you do it, great, but otherwise try doing it by recording yourself telling the story aloud on your phone and play it back to yourself at the end. Thinking a story in our heads is not the same as speaking it aloud and getting to hear our own words spoken.

This is so much harder to do than it sounds. Give it a go, really challenge yourself to stay in the perspective of the other person as you do it. Consider how you feel at the end. Have you changed your mind about what happened or do you feel more right than ever before? The point isn't to change your mind about who was right/wrong of course – the point is to immerse yourself in a very different perspective from the one you have been holding about a situation, to feel how that feels.

Mentalising can be a very playful experience that helps to nurture and develop our capacity for imaginative (re)consideration. It also helps us to read how others might be experiencing us so that we can either keep going as we are or change what/how we are behaving to elicit a different response. It helps to keep us curious, inquisitive and open to being surprised, and if that isn't a playful state of mind, what is?

GET TO KNOW YOUR PLAY PERSONALITY

As a child you probably had a particular type of play that you especially enjoyed, though this didn't stop you from playing in a very broad sense. As we get older, we tend to play in narrower ways, focusing only on the type of play we feel a strong inclination towards or preference for. One way to ensure deeper connections with people in our lives is to ensure we are playfully compatible, and to do that we need to delve a little deeper into our play personality. Dr Stuart Brown discovered, across his extensive research into play across our lifespans, that there are eight general play personalities. You might find that you fit more comfortably into one of these personalities *or* you will, more likely, find that you are a blend of two or three of these.

The Joker: This is where your play tends to revolve around silliness and frivolity. In this play personality, you find your social acceptance by making people laugh. Others will describe you as the practical joker of the group.

The Kinesthete: This play personality centres around movement. You like to move and, moreover, you need to move in order to feel grounded. You like dancing, swimming, walking, yoga and other movement-based activities. You enjoy playing games and sports, but competition is not your motivator – these are just a means of affording you the movement that brings you joy. At your desk, you either have (or should consider having) an exercise ball to sit on instead of a desk chair as the ball will give you movement while you work.

The Explorer: As babies, we discover the world outside ourselves by exploring it. Some of us never stop this. Exploring the world, travelling widely and discovering new places and spaces is your way of engaging with imagination and staying playful. Exploration can be physical (travelling to new places) but can also be emotional (exploring a broader range of emotions and deeper emotional experiences through music and movement) and even a mental experience (exploring new ways to think about or understand something).

The Competitor: This play personality experiences the joy of playing competitive games and always by the rules. If this is you, you play to win and the joy is in the winning. You can play alone, in group activities or even experience joy of being a spectator and feeling joy at your team winning. Winning is the point of playing for you.

The Director: This play personality enjoys planning and hosting activities and events for others. You are a natural organiser, you throw parties and suggest fun outings for the group. When you are on form, you are the centre of everything in a very dynamic and engaged way, but when you are not on form, you can be experienced as more manipulative because what you say goes, no negotiations.

The Collector: The excitement of play for you is that you possess the best collection or the rarest, most coveted items.

The item can be anything from stamps to coins to doll's house furniture to fridge magnets. This can be a fun but solitary activity or you can experience joy in connecting with other collectors who share your passion.

The Artist/Creator: The joy for this play personality is in creating things, be they beautiful things, functional things or random and seemingly pointless things. You might play with painting, sculpting, knitting, taking things apart and reassembling them or even decorating a room or upcycling a piece of furniture. It is all play to you.

The Storyteller: For this play personality, it is all about imagination. These play personalities might well be poets, novelists, illustrators or actors, but equally you may be someone who plays with reading books or watching movies and imagining yourself in the plot, or how you would change the plot to effect a different outcome. You can even find playfulness in a mundane activity… when you are cooking, you imagine you are on *The Great British Bake-Off.*

Whatever your play personality or play tendency is, embrace it. By learning about other play personalities and tendencies, you have choices to try something new, experiment with play and see how it feels for you to do so. How you play does not matter – *that* you play matters! Remember, we are wired *to* play and we are wired *through* play. Play is a relational experience. Through play we learn so much about ourselves but also about ourselves in relation to others. Play enriches relationships and makes us happier and more content.

PLAY BREAK TO GET MENTALISING

This activity is a fun way to playfully stimulate your mentalisation capacity. You will need a play partner (any available and willing adult in your life will do nicely), a pen, a stack of Post-it notes or a couple of sheets of paper (different colours are ideal but if not even different pens/markers will do) and a bowl or container for the bits of paper.

Now, write a number of relatable scenarios on scraps of paper, fold them over and place them in a bowl. These might be statements like: *Jack swears aloud before he throws his phone across the room* or *Alice redials the number again. It rings through to voicemail for the fifth time in a row* or *It is Saturday night and Fiona is curled up on her sofa under a blanket, with a glass of wine in her hand. A handbag, shoes and a coat are thrown in a heap on the floor by the door.* You can make up your own.

Now have two sets of different-coloured paper if you can, or use different-coloured pens to write on plain paper. On one stack (let's say the blue stack) are feeling statements, such as: *He was angry that she... She was angry that he... She was frustrated because her friend... He was upset that he... They were confused about...* On the other (let's say red) stack, write out action statements such as: *He wouldn't listen... He yelled at her... She betrayed him... He lied... She didn't understand... They excluded her...* You can have some additional pieces of information on another stack of papers called PLOT TWISTS. These sit in the middle of the table, and when one of you feels that the other's story could do with a plot twist, hand them the piece of paper and that gives the additional details which they must now adapt their emerging narrative to take into account. First you take turns to read out a starter scenario, and then each person must introduce a feeling and an action statement and incorporate the plot twist. This is a great activity for a group too so consider this one at your next dinner party.

CHAPTER FOUR

Play and Work

A curious mind is a playful mind and will help to unlock creativity and enhance productivity in how we live and also in how we work. We need to bring more playfulness into our work environments and I do not mean highly structured team-building days spent abseiling over the side of ramps or cliffs... or at least not just that. Work is often (mis)understood as being the opposite of play, but that is not how it should be. The work that we find most satisfying and fulfilling tends to be an extension of some activity we enjoyed doing in our childhoods. Dr Stuart Brown conducted over 6,000 play histories with people from a variety of professions (literally everyone from Nobel laureates to incarcerated prisoners) and found that work that is actually a playful experience exists in most settings. For example, he found that architects and engineers who excel in their work but also really enjoy their work tended to have enjoyed playing with blocks and building designs in their childhoods.

In our childhood, the experience of play itself was the reward and we were highly driven towards playful endeavours because play supports our rapidly developing brains in childhood. In adulthood, brain development slows down and so that drive for play is not as active, plus we have been conditioned to relinquish play and become a 'serious grown-up'.

Our decreasing play drive might do us no harm initially in adulthood as we are so focused on our careers and work that we feel we don't need or even have time to play anymore. In the short term, we don't see the full effect of this on our lives – it is when we have cast play aside for a prolonged duration that we lose our spark and joy for life. Our mood drops and we become less optimistic, even struggling to find joy and pleasure in everyday life, which children, masters at the art of play, find so easy to do. But we *can* make up this play deficit and recapture the benefits play affords us. We need to make play a part of our daily routines, like a good night's sleep and drinking two litres of water. Play is as important as a good night's sleep or a healthy diet in terms of its role in our brain's continuing growth and development as well as our ongoing sense of well-being, capacity for adaptation and overall social cohesion.

Our experiences during the pandemic when we were forced to work and play from home with loss of access to our outside resources showed us how these two aspects of our lives can enhance each other.

Once we recapture the value and importance of play in our lives and appreciate what it does for us, we lean in to a greater sense of joy and excitement and we can take a chance on new experiences. This is about working to live, rather than living to work. When we can make our work an extension of our playful lives, we will experience greater levels of fulfilment both at work and away from work.

PLAYFULLY UNDERWHELMING OURSELVES

I mentioned earlier that when we feel a sense of 'stuckness' in our lives it is a sign that we have forgotten to play. I want to pick up on this thread again here but relate it to those times when we are overwhelmed by our work and how play can get us back on track.

I have had a fairly intense workload these last couple of years and had a time-sensitive deadline in recent weeks. I could feel the pressure of it building along with the weight of the demands I was under. As I explored how I could clear my weekend to tackle the workload, I caught myself and thought, *I won't alleviate this stress and pressure by putting myself under yet more stress and pressure to find space to do that.* So, I booked myself onto a half-day calligraphy class for the weekend in question. I played, I explored my creative side and this allowed me to emotionally exhale, and when I did sit down to tackle my project, I met my deadline a lot more comfortably than I would have had I not taken the time to play.

You will know the phrase *All work and no play makes Jack a dull person*. Well, I think that lack of opportunity to play can leave us with an emptiness inside, an internal lack or void that we will seek to fill with less than ideal coping or compensation strategies, such as more work, excessive alcohol, an unhealthy relationship with food, self-injurious or destructive behaviours. When we are working in an area we know we hold expertise and competence in, we tend to enjoy the work more, and when we can enjoy what we are doing, we can approach the process with creativity and playfulness. The problem arises when we stop playing because then our behaviour becomes fixed, rigid and inflexible, leaving us far fewer opportunities to seek and find joy in life and in the world around us. But when we let our playful side express itself across our lifespan, as we are (neurologically) wired to do, we will discover opportunities to play all around us.

When we stop playing, we stop growing as people, and with the short-circuiting of our need to grow and develop as people across our lifespan, things start going off track for us. We can start to feel very disconnected — from ourselves, others and certainly the world, including our work. Play is an embodied experience, and when we stop playing, we feel it in our bodies.

At times, this can feel like a zoning out and not even being aware of our body movements. Have you ever arrived at the door of your destination without realising the journey you took to get there? Have you ever looked up from an absorbing task only to see the time and suddenly realise you haven't eaten or perhaps gone to the toilet for six hours? I am quite sure many if not most of us have, because this kind of body disconnect is common and therefore familiar.

If you can catch yourself in these moments of disconnect you can take a *compassion pause*, whereby you close your eyes for a minute and think: *Have I brought compassionate awareness to my thinking today? Have I brought compassionate awareness to how I am feeling today? Have I brought compassionate awareness to my body today?*

If the answer is no, take a play break and engage in one of the activities scattered throughout this book *or* get outdoors for a couple of minutes because simply getting up from your work space and walking outside changes your field of vision and helps to reset your overwhelmed body and brain. While out there, even for just a couple of minutes, play! When you see a red car, jump up and down three times, and when you see a cyclist, turn around twice. Close your eyes for a minute and listen to all the sounds around you; try to count them, and if you find your mind wandering back to the work you left on your desk, do *the bird practice*, which is that every time you hear a bird you say to yourself *I hear a bird* and it serves to pull you back into the now moment and anchor you down into your body, away from your overwhelmed brain. If you are walking in a more built-up urban area and hearing birds is a tricky task, switch this to *I see a red car/bicycle*, and spotting and naming your talisman will bring you back to the right here, right now. This is about using play to reconnect with ourselves, and it is a very useful form of self-care to defend against overwhelm and burnout.

MINDING YOUR MIND, THE PLAYFUL WAY

Like mindfulness, play is a practice in training the mind to slow down, attune and be grounded in the now moments.

I want to emphasise that I see such mindfulness as a form of therapeutic self-care and a great and very worthwhile investment in ourselves. I do not see mindfulness as a 'cure' or a treatment for mental ill-health. When our mental health is mostly good, playfulness and mindfulness can support it in staying healthy and well, but if you experience mental ill-health, I strongly advise you to consult with a suitably qualified mental-health professional first and foremost. I still advocate playfulness as part of my treatment protocols and clinical work with people, but I do not intend this book to read as a treatment protocol. Mental health is something we all have, and we all experience highs and lows within our mental health. We do not all experience mental ill-health, and those of us who do are deserving of good-quality, responsive care.

Taking care of yourself will enable you to best take what this book and play as a practice can offer you.

My battle cry in this sphere of self-care is that taking time out to play is not an act of frivolity that distracts from your work or other roles but enables you to reach your potential in all areas of your life without compromising your own well-being.

Earlier, when I spoke about understanding our autonomic nervous system, I encouraged you to think about what you tend to do when you are dysregulated. This chapter is about investing in your emotional regulation, strengthening that ventral vagus nerve, which allows you to stay safe and regulated. Taking care of yourself is the best way that you can take care of others in your life.

THE IMPORTANCE OF DOING NOTHING

The cultural demand to be busy and to see busy as a badge of honour can lead to an internalised blind spot when it comes to hearing what it is we actually need to relax and unwind, resulting in us using coping strategies that don't actually help us to release the stress of our busy lives. For some of us this is a reliance on caffeine, food or alcohol that give us a false sense of mobilised energy, encouraging us to push further beyond our limits to get more done. These are temporary coping strategies that give us a false sense of control in anxious times.

When we are in this (un)helpful coping zone, we will also find that we rely on distractions like social media, binge-watching TV or using alcohol to switch off and unwind, even though these are also stimulants that contribute to our emotional exhaustion. It feels like the more stress and pressure we are under, the harder we push ourselves to do more if only to show ourselves and others that we can handle it. But this is *not* how we take control of our lives and serves only to lock us into a state of heightened autonomic nervous system dysregulation whereby we become anxious, irritable and cannot switch off, so we eventually get sick or we dip very low in our autonomic nervous system, becoming depressed and burned out.

Our nervous system feeds off the messages we absorb from our physical and emotional environments and ultimately moves us away from our healthy, regulated baseline. We will all have times when the context demands more from us and we activate to respond to this, but when this stress activation is prolonged, we need to find ways to calm and heal our nervous system. Play is the most effective and available way to achieve this healing because it raises our capacity for emotional resilience and self-regulation in the face of stress.

In these always switched-on times we live in, when we have an endless and constant stream of information available at the touch of a screen, we rarely get the opportunity to just let our minds wander. Try to think of the last time that you just allowed your gaze to stare out of a window while your mind wandered into the reverie of a daydream. It is an increasingly rare phenomena as we are more likely to navel gaze into our phones.

Losing our capacity to be bored is sabotaging our playfulness. Boredom is that free-floating state of reverie when, in the state of nothingness, something new can emerge, such as an idea, a thought, a memory or a feeling. Out of boredom comes desire. Creative people will rarely see boredom as a negative in their lives but will see it as an opportunity to create and discover something that sparks joy for them. Earlier, I wrote about the darker side of play and now I want to highlight boredom as the difficult/challenging part of play.

Living a playful life doesn't mean that we experience only joy in life; it is by living a more playful life that we find the joy in mastering the struggles and challenges life brings our way. We have to move beyond seeing boredom as a sign that we should stop playing and reframe it as a sign that we can playfully push through the discomfort. This interplay of comfort and discomfort is crucial to taking a playful approach to our work lives. We will have difficult tasks and trials within our work lives, we will be under stressful deadlines and pressures, which is *precisely why* we need to ensure that there is space to play in our work lives, so that we can find that pleasure in creatively working through the pressure. If we can embrace it with curiosity and creativity, we move towards a place of seeing that play is our work and our work is play.

Try this activity as a way of seeing a playful challenge as a means of interrupting monotony and routine.

Reroute to reboot: Change how you travel to work one day each week. It may be that you usually travel by bus, but one day a week walk, drive, cycle or go by train. It may be that you always travel the shortest route, but one day a week leave earlier so that you can go the longer way. Look up on a map app the many different potential routes between your starting point and your regular destination.

Challenge yourself to find a new route to travel one day each week. When you do, pay attention to the different things you see, hear, smell. Different people, different signs, buildings, cafes. Is it more or less scenic? Do you feel different when you arrive at where you are going and if so in what ways? Find something new, just one thing will do, that you observed when you rerouted your journey.

Our lives can be frenetically paced and so while this might seem counterintuitive, treat it as a way to kickstart boredom. Schedule time to do nothing. Create space and time to sit and look out of a window. Look at the clouds and find shapes, animals, facial expressions or objects in them.

One way to consciously start to slow ourselves down is to take an activity that we do every day or at least most days. It should be an activity that you take for granted and engage in almost mindlessly. Getting dressed, taking a shower, making or eating a meal, even going to the toilet. The next time you do this activity, slow down and stay as anchored as possible in the now moment, directing all of your focus to the task at hand. Be aware of the feelings in your body, changes in temperature, movement, self-touch, bodily sensations, smell/taste (as applicable). Do you feel relief, satiation, comfort, any shift in awareness of mind or body? For the few minutes (5–15 minutes) the task takes, be as close to 100% mindfully present as possible. Repeated experience of this type of mindful awareness can help us to increase our attunement to how we *feel* in the world around us and to ground us in the *right here, right now* and be less likely to keep scrolling on our phones to sabotage that awareness with distraction.

Approached playfully, boredom is a mindful experience.

THE INTERPLAY OF AWE, WONDER AND BOREDOM

For playfulness to exist and become embedded in our work life, we need to break down what a playful mindful approach to *self-care* is because that helps to prevent professional fatigue or burnout and keep us actively engaged in our work.

Play also helps to challenge and change how we think about concepts such as boredom. Boredom is in short supply in our ever-switched-on, fast-paced lives, but we need boredom because out of boredom, desire emerges. When we can hold that free-floating state of boredom and allow our minds to wander, without sabotaging the experience with distraction (such as mindlessly scrolling on our phones), we will experience new ideas, thoughts, impulses and suggestions as to what else we can do.

Can you imagine how useful this skill could be in your work life? Feel stuck or under-stimulated by a task? Embrace that feeling and see what comes out of it as a means of moving forward. If you find your job boring, reframe such boredom as an opportunity for creativity, ideas, solutions and new ways of approaching the role. Boredom is (potentially) an intellectual play space. A blissful state of daytime reverie is when the mind can wander and wonder via our imaginations, and where new ideas percolate. *Play* at work has to be more than a pool table or pinball machine in the break room.

Wonderment has a dual function and can be expressed as an awe type of response to observing something but also can enable us to consider new possibilities and play with solution-focused thinking, as seen with *I wonder if...* Solution-focused thinking is essential in our work lives as well as our general lives.

Awe is that feeling of being in the presence of something bigger than ourselves that transcends our current understanding of our world. Even the small amount of the awe that is enabled by wonderment can predict our future well-being. When we 'wonder', we are considering an array of possibilities and playing with them. Wonderment is often viewed as being the opposite to rationality, but I would argue that a strong capacity for wonderment affords us the space to explore and evolve in our thought process that will lead us to rationalising what we are doing and how we are doing it. So, do not look on wonderment as a distraction from serious thought and decision-making but as a way to broaden and extend rational thinking.

Play and wonderment are a kind of in-between process that carries us from the co-dependence of childhood to independence in adulthood. Play is the bridge between these different stages of our lives. A playful state of mind helps us to travel the trajectory of our life stages in a smoother and more harmonious way. We never lose that need for play in our lives but we can de-prioritise it as the demands for seriousness increase as we reach adulthood.

When we can play, anything can happen because play makes everything possible. For this reason, play is an extraordinary medium and its presence/absence in our lives and in our world has significant and far-reaching consequences for our physical and emotional well-being and our social functioning. We must play! And it must feel safe to be curious for that playful state of mind to emerge in each of us.

Play promotes social connection at work because when we play together, we attune to each other and this helps to build team cohesion. If we want to work together as a team, we need to start playing together as a team.

Beyond the corporate team-building days of orienteering, abseiling and the like, we also need ways to nurture our playful side so that we might fully engage with these outings when they arise. Developing play strategies that lend themselves to the work environment may need a little planning and structure even when you'd like to be more whimsical. Try these ways to consciously build play breaks into your office world.

MINI PLAY BREAK IDEAS

Create a play space: You might remember how the bell would ring in school signifying time to run outside to play, and another bell would ring signifying the time to line up to come back inside and work again. Well, this type of dedicated daily play space can be a useful way to establish some structured routine to how you play. Ring-fence some time each day (I advocate 15 minutes of play as a daily practice but do what time frame feels right for you) and when it is *that* time, stop what you are doing, put down the phone, turn away from screen devices. Put a song on your earphones and dance, sing, take out a jigsaw or board game or deck of cards, get outdoors

and run or spin around, keep some Play-Doh in a desk drawer
and mould and sculpt with it, take out some Lego blocks and
build something for a few minutes. Make time for play and
then ring-fence that time no matter what else is happening
in the day.

Book a play slot: Book a slot on a climbing wall, a zip line, at
crazy golf or a trampolining centre (for before work, lunchtime
or after work). You can book a solo slot or make a plan to go
with a friend. If you have booked a slot then you know exactly
what is going to happen and when and where it will happen.
Then you turn up and engage. Climbing, getting your feet off
the ground and up into the air, all of it is play.

Perhaps you could book a half-day's leave from work and
spend the afternoon in a museum or, if close by, take a lunch
break in a museum. If you do this, try this little game that I
love to play when I'm in a museum. In each room you enter,
imagine you can choose one piece that you would own (limitless budget here) and think about why you've chosen this piece
and where you would put it in your home – why not create
the imaginary home of your dreams to house these pieces
while you are at it? You can play this alone or with someone.

A sketch a day helps me to play: Get a sketch pad or a notebook with blank pages inside it. Every day, draw something. It

doesn't matter what it is or how it looks, but draw something. This can be your daily play activity and it is all contained in your notebook. Here are some playful art activity suggestions to help you further structure and frame this one:

- *Colour your feelings:* Start by deciding what colour each feeling is, see each one as a shape, different sizes, textures. Now when you have a red blobby day, a small purple triangle type of day or a blue spikey day, only you know what it means, but you can colour those out in your notebook.

- *Colour a thought:* Think of a variety of colours and, holding each colour in your mind one at a time (or a different colour each day), set yourself a task to *Think a blue thought while you colour blue on the page. What are you thinking and how do you feel about that thought?* and repeat with other colours. When you consider what a blue/red/green/orange/purple thought might be, hold the thought in mind, draw it as a shape, colour it in, small or big on the page.

- Map it out: Take a page and, holding a pencil in your dominant hand, close your eyes and move the pencil around the page to make the outline of your map (add a section to close the lines when you open your eyes). Now for 15 minutes each day, add something to your map (houses, transport, recreational aspects, people, infrastructure, environmental features) to create your perfect world/community.

Paint stones: Next time you are out for a walk near a beach, gather up some small smooth stones/shells and keep them in your desk drawer with a small paintbrush set. Spend 15 minutes painting a stone. You can keep your work or write messages of kindness and compliments on the back and leave them in random places for others to discover and enjoy.

None of this should be confused with skiving off or not taking your work seriously. Nurturing your capacity for mentalisation, embracing opportunities to mind-wander and making time for boredom while building in mini play breaks in your day is precisely what will drive your creativity, solution-focused thinking and critical-thinking faculties in general. It will allow you to generate new ideas and ways of doing things and ultimately make you a happier, more well-rounded and productive member of the team.

Drawing on the more creative parts of your brain is very useful in the workplace even if, and perhaps especially if, yours is not a particularly creative role. Immersing one part of your brain in intense cognitive, cerebral activity can lead to a staleness in your efforts. However, mixing it up and engaging the more creative and playful part of your brain at regular intervals allows you to become more adaptable to changes in your role and in the work environment. It will keep your energy levels higher and increase job satisfaction.

PLAY BREAK

Play to unlock creativity

Creativity is a commodity in our working lives. No matter what line of business you are in, you are creating something, be it a product, a solution, a message, a service or a new idea, and you rely on creativity. This is why corporate organisations bring someone like me in to get their staff playing. You've likely heard the phrase that *necessity is the mother of all invention*, and as I said at the start of this book, play isn't just nice, it is necessary. Moreover, play is the mother of creativity and the invention that flows from that creativity. Playful people create!

A nice way to use play to pull ourselves from a seriousness slump into a more creative reverie is surrealism art.

If you have a newspaper or magazine around the house, take it now and find a photo in it. With a pen, deface the photo to transform it into a surreal portrait. Exaggerate the features; add features or objects to the photo to create something new. Surrealism is about playing with how something 'should' look in accordance with the real world; it's about combining features and objects that enable us to play with the order of things. You are combining the everyday (the norm) with the bizarre or unusual to produce something silly and surreal and, in its own way, very beautiful. You can do this with photos as well but you might not want to permanently deface a photo and, as such, a picture in a newspaper or magazine might feel more accessible to you. You could also source and print out a famous sculpture or painting and recreate this using your surreal approach.

Try cutting the heads out of photos of celebrities in magazines. Transfer the heads onto bodies of (photos of) animals or switch and put the animal head in the place of the celebrity head. Now develop an identity and background story for your new character. Combine a collection of such creations on a blank page and develop the story further.

You could also draw this out. Bring to mind an everyday item such as a cup, a phone or shoes and in drawing them, add something unusual – draw a dog wearing shoes and a hat, turn a mobile phone into a hamster and imagine making calls or sending texts on your hamster phone. Draw what this new phone handset looks like. Draw a shoe drinking a cup of tea.

Tip: I cut out and collect images I think might be fun to do this with as I see them. I keep them in an envelope or a box so that when I feel the urge to play and to engage with my creative side, I have my supplies ready to go.

WORKING AT OUR PLAYFUL SIDE

Sometimes, when we think of who or what a playful person is, just one type springs to mind. Someone who is hyperactive, always messing around and laughing, takes nothing seriously and dresses in brightly coloured playful clothes, with blue hair. We might want to pause and wonder where we got the impression that playful adults look like a mid-1980s kids' TV presenter! Is it to reassure ourselves that the reason we don't pause to make time for play is because it simply isn't our style/ persona? *I am not a playful person because I don't look playful and I have a serious job* is more of a statement of defence than a statement of truth.

In fact, playful people experience this regulatory roller-coaster with waves of high physical and emotional energy followed by periods of quieter and softer energy. This capacity is largely what enables an ongoing playful state of mind without resources getting depleted. It means that such people can seem enthusiastic and engaged even when overtly passive. Self-regulation means that we can be ruled internally rather than by the demands of an external work schedule. It is about knowing when to release and when to replenish in equal measure. This is precisely how play resources resilience.

The active and mobilising aspect of play is about rhythm and activity, whereas the downtime is enabling necessary reflection to keep us anchored in that safe and regulated space within our nervous system. When we inaccurately view playfulness as ridiculousness, we can mistakenly assume playful people are jokers, not as bright intellectually as more overtly serious people, the class clown if you will, overcompensating with humour. In truth, playful people hold that space of open curiosity, eager to better understand situations, projects and people without assuming they already know all of the answers. For me, this is the definition of being 'smart' and serves to remind us that there are many types of intelligence and thinking in our world, and all of them serve a very valuable contribution.

The same can be said to any assertion that playfulness goes hand in hand with immaturity. A certain amount of immaturity can enable fresh insights (all fuelled by the flexibility, creativity and curiosity of the playful mind) because a playful mind remains open to new thinking and perspective on matters. Playful people are also disciplined and highly principled people. It takes persistence and perseverance to sustain a playful state of mind; giving up can feel a lot easier.

Convergent thinking is related to IQ tests and rational thought with solution-focused thinking where there is a clear-cut singular answer. Divergent thinking, on the other hand, is related to coming up with a slew of answers and ideas to a situation along with the flexibility to adapt from one path to a solution to another, by taking other perspectives and changing circumstances into account. A truly playful state of mind will reflect evidence of both convergent and divergent thinking and, moreover, the flexibility to switch from one form of thinking smoothly to another. These are the type of thinkers we *need* to be in our work lives.

Play is part of my job and it is also part of my personality, so it is both *who* I am as well as *what I do*. I don't think that I could work in the field of play (I am in both play practice and research fields) without my playful state of mind. But because it is my job, it is also work, and like any other form of work, that requires dedication, study, training, learning and dogged perseverance.

What do you think is the most common thing people say to me when they hear what I do for a living? *Oh, you get to play with kids all day – that must be so nice and so much fun.* I get the thinking behind that, I truly do. It is so nice to think that jobs that involve high levels of creativity are, at least mostly, fun-focused. And, of course, there is fun – I love what I do and feel privileged that I get to do it. But the role that play serves in my work is very different from how I engage with play in my life. I am using play to effect change in someone's psyche in my work, and we sit with the darkness of this as much as the light. This is play with purpose, and mindful play with therapeutic goals. In my life, I play to release and recover, I play to connect. In both areas, I play with purpose, and at times that playfulness requires more perseverance and is more work than it is at other times.

In many ways, the essence of playfulness is to stretch beyond our current reality to create a new one, a new way of doing things.

Sometimes when you try to become more playful in work you find that the environment isn't all that playful. This doesn't mean that play isn't possible in your work, but it does mean that getting to that place will be more challenging from where you are right now.

Consider what your work is and what parts of the job align with who you are and how you want to be and what parts don't. Have you ever imagined yourself working in another setting that would spark more joy for you? This allows you to imagine what your dream job would be if you could choose absolutely anything to do. Do it now. I tend to fantasise about working in a book shop or a library, surrounded by books and reading all day... blissful, right? Realistic? Not at all. If you speak to someone who does your fantasy job they will tell you about the mundanity, the tedium, the challenges within that job too. Imagining your dream job doesn't depend on the practicality and realism of such a choice right now in your life. It's a fantasy – it doesn't need to be real.

Imagining and fantasising during childhood helped to build your mental repertoire and you can (re)activate those parts of your brain now as an adult. Through playful and imaginative practice, your brain will filter and provide a shape to your fantasy to better fit what is possible in reality anyway, *but* this can only happen as a result of a more playful state of mind. So give way to the fantasy for now, as it serves a very important function for our brain development. There may even be ways to take the fantasy aspects of the job and apply them to our lives aside from work. For me, I joined a book club, and while we do read books, we rarely read the same ones at the same time. We don't always discuss books in great depth, but we gather, we eat, we drink, we share, we laugh, we solve all of the problems in the world and we connect... we play. Anything that brings you increased access to connection, shared joy and playfulness should be pursued with the vigour and seriousness of a new job you want. This is part of the serious joy of play.

There are always new or alternative ways of doing things in life. It doesn't mean that they are always easy to find and, as such, we benefit from a playful approach to help us to engage the kind of creativity and flexibility required to make any change possible.

Play doesn't solve all of the challenges we will face in our work life, nor does it prevent some of those problems from arising. What play does is afford us a fresh perspective on how we engage with problems and challenges in our work. It fuels creativity and innovation while strengthening connection with colleagues, and creates a safer and more emotionally containing work environment. From this space, we experience the problems and challenges that come our way in the work environment not as a block but as an invitation to creatively flow through them.

With a more playful approach to our work life, we build an environment where people feel their needs are understood and met and are enabled to understand and meet the needs of others in return. This is why I advocate that we create work spaces for ourselves that enable us to stay play-hydrated.

PLAY BREAK

Word it out to work it out

Try this quick word-play game to engage your critical thinking and problem-solving skills.

Starting with one word, change only one letter at a time to arrive at a different word in four to six steps.

Example: From Head to Tail

Head

Heal

Teal

Teil

Tail

Now try to get from SEAM to MEAT or create one such list yourself. Sometimes it will work out and sometimes it won't, but it is a good way to engage solution-focused thinking nonetheless.

CONCLUSION

Play Is for Life

We have taken a journey through the theory and research of play to its practical role in all aspects of our adult lives and I hope that by now you are at least open and curious about how you can practically embed play into your everyday life. The activities included will, I hope, nudge you towards putting this into action. *Good enough is good enough*, so start small and grow your play intentions from there. This has been about busting that myth that play is for children. Play is for all of us, always!

I started this book by saying that I think that we *all* have the capacity for play and to be playful. This doesn't mean that this is easy for all of us. Our relationship with play is our story – it speaks to our experience of being children and of being parented. And it is worth repeating that while we are storied people, living storied lives, we can also change the stories that we live by. I hope this book has helped to show you how accessible play is. We can talk about growing up in a culture of play, but play *is* culture. So, if we want to change, we need to reflect on the role of play in our lives and actively seek opportunities to increase playfulness.

As we are trained to renounce play, silliness and the chaos of creativity in adulthood, we develop what Hungarian psycho-analyst Sándor Ferenczi called a *confusion of tongues* whereupon adults and children appear to speak the same language but are, in truth, separated by a cognitive and emotional chasm that renders a permanent state of misunderstanding. A child cannot possibly know the mind of an adult, and as adults we have been taught to forget the experience of the child's mind. If culture is *the way we do things* then play sits in among the things we do/do not do.

Play is a key part of how we position and understand ourselves in relation to others and the world around us. If culturally we adults have been conditioned to see play as an enterprise for children alone then it is time to change the culture of play. It is precisely through experimenting, exploring and deepening our insights into play that we discover new or hidden depths to ourselves. Play is the route to our fullest potential because it fuels the flexibility and adaptability we need to successfully and happily negotiate life and everything it will throw at us, while unlocking our capacity for shared joy and authentic connection within ourselves as well as with others and the world around us. Increased playfulness in all of our lives replenishes the resources we need in order to become emotionally resilient people, which does not mean stressful events will not stress us out (they most certainly will) but we will have the resources we need to feel our way through those stressful experiences and emerge from them.

I hope that you have read this book as a reflection on your personal play patterns and as a roadmap to the playful life you want to lead. The world is full of humour and opportunities for play. Expose yourself to these by pausing to observe play in action, feel how others play and start with small things like throwing a ball for a dog or joining a young child on the floor in their play experience.

It is okay to be a beginner in this play process, even as an adult, so embrace opportunities to learn from others and gradually build up your own capacity for silliness, and if silliness feels out of reach, start with structured play activities. Whatever you do, become more active in your pursuit of play, dance to a song in the privacy of your own home or add a subtle little bounce to your walk every time you see a blue car drive by. Easing yourself into play might feel safer, and remember that it must feel safe before play is possible. Practise play, daily where possible, but you can also start weekly and increase to every day. Invite playful people into your life and take their lead and start side-lining/minimising the role of those in your life who dampen your play spirit. You might have to try your hand at a variety of play activities to find the one that feeds your play appetite, but you will never regret taking the time to do this.

You get to decide what feels playful for you because it is not the activity that is playful, it is our internal experience of engaging in the activity that decides if it is a playful experience for us. An investment in play is an investment in ourselves and in a happier life.

Starting small and adding something in to each day is a great beginning, so set your 15 minutes per day play goal and start a large jigsaw, buy a fun board game like Hungry Hippos or Twister (need a play partner), Buck-a-Roo, Operation (can play solo), or an adult Lego set (those are expensive though so you can also get basic Lego and create something yourself without the instruction manual by adding a set number of additional blocks each day). Instead of collapsing on the sofa and losing your evening in TV (not devaluing that by the way – we can all benefit from powering down and zoning out sometimes for a short while), gift yourself 15 minutes to play each day before you reach for the remote control.

Consider ways that you can instil more playfulness into your daily work. Using the principle that play strengthens curiosity and encourages experimentation and investigation (of space, objects, relationships, the self), take something that you do daily in work. If you would typically google something you are looking for, this time go to the library to look it up or phone a friend (as that gameshow says) and ask them what they think instead. Find a new, non-internet way of discovering something that also puts you into connection with other adults.

If there is something you have always wanted to try, something you have always had an interest in but have never acted upon, now is the time to do it. Whatever it is, find the way to activate it and get playing.

Don't see embracing play as turning away from our modern, fast-paced world. Actually, embracing play is what will enable us to engage in the ever-and-quick-changing world we live in. We live in a world where skills such as resilience, creativity, adaptability, flexibility are more important than ever before. Play fuels innovation and opens up new possibilities and ways to do things.

Play is all around us – we have to allow ourselves to slow down and engage with these invitations to play because play *really matters*, and my intention in writing this book was to illustrate this point while offering practical ways to kickstart your more playful life.

IF YOU MUST PLAN, PLAN PLAYFULLY

I hope that you have read this book as an invitation to play. I wanted to provide practical ways in which you can flex your play muscles and get play-fit again by taking a chance on a new and sometimes slightly silly way of doing things because play is spontaneous, chaotic, messy, relational, flexible/adaptable (structured), enables mistakes and stretches us a little beyond our so-called comfort zone (can be a discomfort zone too).

Play and spontaneity can complement each other very nicely, but as adults, some of us will need to schedule *some* of our playfulness to ensure we create the space and time for it, and the spontaneity will emerge within that space. Some of us will also struggle to feel creative when in a more shut-down withdrawal state and as such will benefit from some forward planning. Planning can still feel playful and fuel the desired flexibility and adaptability a playful state of mind needs.

If we want to live a more playful life, one that is also more meaningful and one where we feel more connected to those around us, we must create space for play in our lives.

Try this next exercise to explore the time you allocate to different areas of your life.

Life balance wheel: Draw a circle (a wheel) and divide it up into segments that best describe the amount of time/focus or level of priority each of the following have currently in your life. Assign a colour to each one so that you can shade in your wheel accordingly.

- Education/personal development
- Friendships
- Family
- Fun stuff/play
- Work
- Romance
- New experiences
- Relaxation time.

When you have drawn and completed your wheel, pause to consider how it makes you feel. Are you happy with the amount of time and focus you are giving to each area of your life? Could there be more room for play/fun in your life? Where could you pull back on to create the extra time and space you need? This is why the wheel is helpful. We have finite resources so we need to make conscious and mindful choices as to how we deploy them in our lives.

This mindful approach to play and investing in playfulness in our lives is not simply an answer to a problem. It is something that needs to be an active part of how we live our lives to help defend against compassion fatigue and burnout.

When we can prioritise self-care in our lives, we develop that deeper listening capacity. It starts with listening to ourselves so that we can invest in that healing power of being heard. This is compassionate listening and it enables us to express ourselves in a way that provides relief from distress or dysregulation.

Making a compassion commitment like this to ourselves is also an investment in the internal resources of our resilience. Resilience is one of those concepts that tends to be causally discussed and assumed as an automatic thing that some of us have, some of us don't and if we could all just 'be resilient' we would be okay. This is just not how it works. Resilience only exists when our stressors do not outweigh our resources to cope with the matter at hand. It is a constant balancing act and something we have to regularly check in about with ourselves because those levels can rise and dip in different situations. This is why prioritising self-care and actively pursuing opportunities for playfulness in our lives is a radical and necessary act for each of us.

Try this simple activity to kickstart your commitment to play.

Activity jar: Get a jar and write lots of different activity ideas on coloured note paper and fold these up to put inside the jar. These can be anything you think of on any day. Those times when you wistfully say, 'Oh, I must do that someday,' write it down and put it in your jar. Then when you feel you need to get up, out and do something, simply reach into your jar, pull out a random activity and off you go to do that, whatever it might be.

A LETTER FROM JOANNA

I want to say a huge thank you for choosing to read my book. If you did enjoy it and want to keep up to date with all my latest releases, just sign up at the following link. Your email address will never be shared, and you can unsubscribe at any time.

www.thread-books.com/joanna-fortune

When I wrote my 15-Minute Parenting series of books I was used to being asked, 'Why 15 minutes?' and now it is, 'Adults don't really "play" though, do they?' And my answer is a resounding yes. We do play, and moreover we need to play just as young children and teenagers need to play. Play allows us to live in a way that will lead to *fewer tears and more laughter*, regardless of our age.

Play is not an exact science, but researchers from every point of the scientific compass do agree that play is an essential and biological process that has evolved over eons in a way that makes us smarter and more adaptable to change while fostering the development of empathy and connection with others. Humans are the most playful of all species. We live to play, and play enables us to live a fully lived life. This is why I really wanted to spotlight the possibility and moreover the transformative power of play in our adult lives, because I believe play and playful connection to be very important, yet under-discussed, aspects of adult life.

I hope you loved my book and if you did I would be very grateful if you could write a review. I'd love to hear what you think, and it makes such a difference helping new readers to discover one of my books for the first time.

I love hearing from my readers – do get in touch on my social media, Goodreads or my website.

Thanks and remember – play is a state of mind and a way of being, regardless of age, so make time for play!

Joanna

@ImJoannaFortune

www.solamh.com

@joannafortune

Joanna Fortune

RESOURCES

The play list – Some additional 'play-spiration' to get you going on your play journey

START SMALL AND GROW

Embrace opportunities for play by starting small

- If you have children, play with them. Sit and observe and ask if you can join their play. Be aware if you are joining in that does not mean that you are directing their play.
- Take time to daydream. Promise yourself that you will not scroll through your phone when you are sitting over coffee or on public transport. Look around you, out of a window and allow your mind to wander.
- When you make eye contact with someone, even a stranger fleetingly, smile. Take opportunities to smile and laugh wherever you can find them.
- Start saying yes! When someone wonders if you have time for a coffee, want to get out of the office for

lunch, grab a quick drink after work, fancy coming along to tag-rugby to check it out, say yes. None of these is a huge commitment and if not for you, they are boundaried activities that can end when you feel ready to leave.

- Get wondering! Every time you are doing something, no matter how mundane, simply pause and take a couple of minutes to wonder how else it could be done. For example:

  1. Making a cup of coffee – make it hot, iced, black, with milk, use an alternative milk, add a sweetener, use a French press, a cafetière.
  2. Making a cup of tea – make it hot, iced, with milk, lemon, sweetened or not, in a cup or in a pot.
  3. Now try it with any of the following and add your own: tying a tie/knotting a scarf/carrying a handbag/ buttoning up a coat.

Have you ever tried... Now try it!

- Baking (something you don't already know by heart) without recipe instructions.
- Going somewhere new without a map.
- Origami without instructions.
- Knitting without a pattern.
- Painting a picture without a brush.

- Posting a crisp to someone in the hopes (therefore you must try to create a method that means) that it will arrive unbroken. This one came out of a very fun discussion with a group of friends on a night out and there were so many playful solutions to explore and try.

Don't sweat the small stuff, play with it

Use household items such as:

- Paper
- Newspaper
- Kitchen roll
- Cardboard inserts of toilet roll
- Soap (a bar could be used or washing-up-liquid-type soap)
- Clothes pegs
- Paper cups
- Dried pasta
- Bottle tops
- Wine corks
- Leaves/grass cuttings/flowers/twigs.

Craft items such as:

- Sellotape
- String

- Glue (glue stick/PVA glue/hot glue gun – whatever you have)
- Cocktail sticks/matchsticks
- Scissors
- Paint/brush
- Play-Doh.

Make miniature versions of:

- A boat (it must float)
- A windmill with moving sails
- A castle
- A telescope
- A tower
- A crown
- A pirate hat
- A tree
- An animal (go as creative and prehistoric as you like with this one)
- A robot
- A rocket
- A house
- A wreath
- A person.

Everything must be in miniature so that it fits comfortably in the palm of your hand.

GIVE YOURSELF OPTIONS

Play sticks

Get a packet of lollipop sticks (affordable and easily available in any craft shops or if you have children, raid their craft kits). Separate them into three piles of approximately ten each (in truth, you can have as many as you like or even add to these over time). Now you can colour each pile a different colour. You can paint them, use markers, spray paint... whatever you wish and whatever is easiest for you. Let them dry before taking a black pen/marker/sharpie and writing something on each one.

Blue pile: This is your Get Outdoors pile and you will write on these things like:

- Walk a new route.
- Find a tree to climb.
- Stay outside until you see/hear three birds.
- Go to the beach and write your name in the sand.
- Find a red leaf, brown leaf, green leaf.
- Every time you see a cyclist, pause and salute.

Yellow pile: This is your Stay Indoors pile and you will write on these things like:

- Bake fairy cakes but add one new unusual ingredient (can be a decorative one or a flavour one).

- Make a den (using household items like chairs, blankets, cushions, umbrellas, broomsticks, clothes pegs) in your sitting room and lie in it to read your book.

- Get the biggest sheet of paper you can (this may mean raiding the printer paper and sellotaping a number of sheets together to make a big one – that is perfectly okay). Paint your hands and make handprints across the page, rinse them and paint the soles of your feet and walk up and down the sheet of paper. Have a basin of warm soapy water on the floor and treat yourself to a nice foot soak afterwards. Once dry, take a sharpie and turn your prints into faces and add some speech bubbles imaging what they might say to each other.

- Write someone special in your life a letter and post it to them – even if you live with them, because everyone likes to receive personal post.

- Lip-synch by playing your favourite songs and miming singing along (but with full-on actions and emotions conveyed) using a household item (shoe, hairbrush, wooden spoon, etc.) as a microphone – you *need* a microphone.

- Call someone on the phone who you haven't spoken to in ages.

Pink pile: These can be nice, indulgent, treat-style activities (whatever that means to you):

- Run a hot bubble bath and play some relaxing music while you soak.
- Order your favourite takeout and watch your favourite movie.
- Have a duvet day and stay in bed with snacks, books, some TV.
- Dress up in an outfit that makes you feel both fancy and positive about yourself... even if it is 'too much' for the day.
- Apply for your dream job in your dream organisation (regardless of whether they are recruiting or you are exactly qualified for it).
- That thing you have been coveting but couldn't justify buying... buy it.

You can and should write your own as per your tastes and what is fun and indulgent for you. Next time when you are feeling a little flat and want to motivate yourself to do something, simply choose an activity stick based on whether you want to go out, stay indoors or feel pampered and indulge in some needed self-care.

SENSORY SLOW DOWN

Ice-cube surprise

Take an ice-cube tray and place a small piece of Lego into each cube, fill the tray with water and freeze it. Do this with two or even three ice-cube trays if you have them. Each day take a basin/bowl and half fill it with tepid or lukewarm water. Take out two ice cubes each day and sit, holding one ice cube in each hand and submerge your closed fists into the bowl of water. Now wait for the ice to melt. You will have a deep sensory experience by feeling the cold ice in your hands and the warm water on your skin but further, the waiting for the ice to melt is a great way to slow you down, calm and regulate impulses and take you out of your head and into the now moments in your body. If sitting waiting in silence is too much for you, try playing some relaxing music (again whatever that means for you) softly in the room you are in while you wait for the ice cubes to melt. When you have waited, you are rewarded with the two pieces of Lego. Make this your play activity of choice at the end of each day and slowly attach each Lego block to another and create a structure that changes and evolves each day with the addition of new blocks.

Silent disco for one: Stand in a comfortable space (home, garden, bathroom) and play your favourite song, that one song we all have that no matter where we are when it comes on, we just have to dance. Wear your headphones, turn up the volume, close your eyes and just dance as big and wild as you can for the duration of your song. Hopefully a song immediately comes to mind for you. Mine is always Billy Idol's 'Dancing with Myself', so if you ever see me shimmying on a walk or shoulder dancing in my car, that is what I am listening to!

Wander to wonder: While out for a walk, listen to some music and adjust your movement in keeping with the tempo. You don't have to dance down the road (though feel free if the urge grabs you) but I am suggesting you change your gait a bit. Take big steps, small steps, add in a hop, bounce or a skip every now and then. Moving our physical body in different ways can help to move some held thoughts and feelings through us.

WHEN ALL ELSE FAILS, HAVE A WORD WITH YOURSELF!

Talk with yourself: Literally have a conversation with yourself, out loud, as though you were your own best friend talking to you. What would your best friend say to you, want you to hear and know about yourself, encourage you to do. Say it all, out loud. This can be a couple of minutes, even start with one minute and gradually grow it. Yes, it will feel a little weird when you start doing it, but what's wrong with that?

Now, just as you have embraced this idea allow me to stretch you a little beyond your comfort zone. Take this activity on the road with you. When you are out walking, sitting on public transport, walking around the supermarket, strike up this conversation with yourself.

If your eyebrows just shot right up into your hairline, take a breath with me and put a set of earphones into your ears so it will look as though you are taking a phone call and giving this self-esteem smoothie style of feedback to a friend and not yourself. Try it three times before you shrug this one off as not being for you.

The first time will definitely feel strange, perhaps a little exciting with a spark of self-conscious and nervous energy to it. So, this time is not the one to truly assess if this works for you. Give everything three good tries before deciding if it is for you or not and hold in an open mind that while it may not be for you *at this time* in your life, you can keep it in reserve for when you feel differently.

I love observing children chatting away out loud to themselves while they are immersed in their playful reverie. I admire that free abandon they embrace so un-self-consciously. That is what inspired me to try talking out loud to myself for the first time.

FURTHER READING

Research papers cited in this text

Bennett, M.P. & Lengacher, C. (2008). 'Humor and laughter may influence health: III. Laughter and health outcomes.' *Evidence-Based Complementary and Alternative Medicine*, 5(1):37–40. doi: 10.1093/ecam/nem041.

Bennett, M.P., Zeller, J.M., Rosenberg, L. & McCann, J. (2003). 'The effect of mirthful laughter on stress and natural killer cell activity.' *Alternative Therapies in Health and Medicine*, 9(2):38–45.

Boehm, K. & Kubzansky, L. (2012). 'The heart's content: The association between positive psychological well-being and cardiovascular health.' *Psychological Bulletin*, 138(4): 655–691.

Duke, M., Fivush, R. & Lazarus, A. (2008). 'Knowledge of family history as a clinically useful index of psychological well-being and prognosis: A brief report.' *Psychotherapy* (Chicago, IL), 2008–06, 45(2): 268–272.

Ferenczi, S. (1949). 'Confusion of the Tongues Between the Adults and the Child—The Language of Tenderness and of Passion.' *The International Journal of Psychoanalysis*, 30: 225–230.

Luft, J. & Ingham, H. (1955). The Johari Window: A Graphic Model for Interpersonal Relations. University of California Western Training Lab.

Luksevicius de Moraes, Y. *et al.* (2021). 'Adult playful individuals have more long- and short-term relationships.' *Evolutionary Human Sciences*, 3: 1–18.

Proyer, R.T. (2017a). 'A multidisciplinary perspective on adult play and playfulness.' *International Journal of Play*, 6(3): 241–243. Doi:10.1080/21594937.2017.1384307.

Proyer, R.T. (2017b). 'A new structural model for the study of adult playfulness: Assessment and exploration of an understudied individual differences variable.' *Personality and Individual Differences*, 108: 113–122. Doi: 10.1016/j.paid.2016.12.011.

Proyer, R.T. (2019). 'Adult playfulness and relationship satisfaction: An APIM analysis of romantic couples.' *Journal of*

Research in Personality, 79: 40–48. https://doi.org/10.1016/j. jrp.2019.02.001.

United Nation's World Happiness Report: https://worldhappiness.report/ed/2022.

Van Fleet, M. & Feeney, B. (2015). 'Play behaviour and playfulness in adulthood.' *Social and Personality Psychology Compass*, 9/11 (2015): 630–643, 10.1111/spc3.12205

Books cited in this text

Brown, S. (2010). *Play: How it Shapes the Brain, Opens the Imagination and Invigorates the Soul.* New York: Penguin.

Bruner, J. (1986). *Actual Minds, Possible Worlds.* Cambridge MA: Harvard University Press.

Dana, D. (2018). *The Polyvagal Theory in Therapy*. New York: Norton & Co.

Dana, D. (2020). *Polyvagal Exercises for Safety and Connection.* New York: Norton & Co.

Fortune, J. (2020a). *15-Minute Parenting 0–7 Years: Quick and Easy Ways to Connect With Your Child.* Thread Books.

Fortune, J. (2020b). *15-Minute Parenting 8–12 Years: Stress-Free Strategies for Nurturing Your Child's Development.* Thread Books.

Fortune, J. (2020c). *15-Minute Parenting the Teenage Years: Creative Ways to Stay Connected With Your Teenager.* Thread Books.

Freud, S. (1901/1991). *The psychopathology of everyday life.* London: Penguin.

Panksepp, J. (2004). *Affective Neuroscience.* Oxford: Oxford University Press.

Porges, S. & Dana, D. (2018). *Clinical Applications of the Polyvagal Theory.* New York: Norton & Co.

Saltzberg, B. (2010). *Beautiful Oops!* New York: Workman Publishing.

Sinclair, V. (2016). *Switching Mirrors.* Stockholm: Trapart Books.

Online resources cited in this text

Brown, S. (2008). 'Play is more than just fun.' TED talk. www.ted.com/talks/stuart_brown_play_is_more_than_just_fun?language=en.

Fortune, J. (2017). 'Social Media – the ultimate shame game?' TEDx Talk https://youtu.be/ORhwrL71dYc.

Keane, J. (sex educator) www.jennykeane.com.

Panksepp, J. (2014). *The science of emotions.* TEDxRainier event. www.youtube.com/watch?v=65e2qScV_K8.

Rory's Story Cubes https://www.storycubes.com/en/

Books to reconnect with fairy tales

Bettleheim, B. (1976/1991). *The Uses of Enchantment – the meaning and importance of fairy tales.* London: Penguin Random House.

Brothers Grimm. *Little Red Riding Hood.*

Carter, A. (1990). *The Bloody Chamber.* London: Penguin.

Sullivan, D. (2017). *Tangleweed and Brine.* Dublin: Little Island Books.

Warner, M. (2014). *Once Upon a Time – A short history of fairy tale.* Oxford: Oxford University Press.

ACKNOWLEDGEMENTS

I want to thank my wonderful agent, Marianne Gunn-O'Connor, who is so encouraging and supportive and always sees the biggest picture and endless potential in what I do.

I want to thank my editor Claire Bord, who has always embraced 15-Minute Parenting and the concept of a more playful life in its fullest terms. It would not be possible for me to put my beliefs, thoughts and ideas into writing without someone like Claire who can listen to me talk and transform a conversation into a book proposal.

I want to thank the entire Thread team for the creative and playful ways they have amplified my work and opened it up to a much wider audience.

I want to thank all of you who have read this book, my other books, listened to my podcast and radio show and engaged with me on social media with your own thoughts, ideas and wonderings. Every time you post about the books or podcast or share them with friends you become part of the 15-Minute Parenting/Play community.

I want to acknowledge the support and encouragement I received from my doctorate supervisor, Dr Rupert King, who helped to ground me as I was editing my thesis and writing this book at the same time. This support ensured that I could hold a boundary around each separate piece of work.

I want to thank my friends and family members, my cheerleaders and advocates for everything I do. I am so grateful to be part of such a playful group of people and for the containing spaces of shared joy and ideas we enjoy together.

And by no means least, my endlessly supportive husband, Diarmuid, and my ambassador of play, Maisie, without whom none of this would ever have come to fruition. Every time I have said, 'This is the last book I will write,' my husband has smiled knowingly, anticipating that there was more to be said.

This book was written in a time of global pandemic and doctorate deadlines. It afforded me a playful headspace at a time when I really needed it, and I hope that it does the same for all of you who pick it up.